"An ideal combination of solid research with practical, devotional, pastoral insight—enjoyable and edifying to read. Articulating the demands of the kingdom, Storms challenges us to live for God's heart and to trust his faithfulness."

—Craig Keener, Professor of New Testament, Palmer Seminary; author, *The NIV Application Commentary: Revelation*

"If you want meditations that will lift your mind to the majesty of God and the supremacy of his Son, if you want devotionals that come out of the biblical text and not someone's imagination, if you want reflections on especially difficult topics such as suffering, then this book is for you. Storms embraces the truth of the biblical text in a trustworthy and uplifting manner."

—Bill Mounce, President, BiblicalTraining.org

"Sam Storms is one of the most intelligent, incisive, and eloquent Bible teachers of the early twentieth-first century. I heard him teach a class on Revelation 2 and 3 and found it to be one of the most intellectually stimulating and spiritually transformational Bible classes I have ever attended. The good news is that his teaching on the letters to the seven churches is now available to everyone. People who read this book will be drawn closer to the Lord by this Christ-centered and Spirit-anointed teacher."

—Lyle W. Dorsett, Billy Graham Professor of Evangelism, Beeson Divinity School

To the One Who
CONQUERS

Crossway books by Sam Storms:

Chosen for Life: The Case for Divine Election
The Hope of Glory: 100 Daily Meditations on Colossians
Signs of the Spirit: An Interpretation of Jonathan Edwards's
Religious Affections

To the One Who
CONQUERS

50 Daily Meditations
on the Seven Letters of Revelation 2–3

Sam Storms

CROSSWAY BOOKS

WHEATON, ILLINOIS

To the One Who Conquers: 50 Daily Meditations on the Seven Letters of Revelation 2–3
Copyright © 2008 by Enjoying God Ministries
Published by Crossway Books
      a publishing ministry of Good News Publishers
      1300 Crescent Street
      Wheaton, Illinois 60187

Cover design: Jon McGrath
Cover illustration: IStock
Design and typsetting: Lakeside Design Plus
First printing 2008

Unless otherwise indicated, Scripture quotations are from *The Holy Bible, English Standard Version®*, copyright © 2001 by Crossway Bibles, a publishing ministry of Good News Publishers. Used by permission. All rights reserved.

Scripture quotations marked NASB are from *The New American Standard Bible®*. Copyright © The Lockman Foundation 1960, 1962, 1963, 1968, 1971, 1972, 1973, 1975, 1977, 1995. Used by permission.

Scripture references marked NIV are from *The Holy Bible: New International Version®*. Copyright © 1973, 1978, 1984 by International Bible Society. Used by permission of Zondervan Publishing House. All rights reserved.

    The "NIV" and "New International Version" trademarks are registered in the United States Patent and Trademark Office by International Bible Society. Use of either trademark requires the permission of International Bible Society.

All emphases in Scripture quotations have been added by the author.

Trade paperback ISBN: 978-1-4335-0138-8
PDF ISBN: 978-1-4335-0454-9
Mobipocket ISBN: 978-1-4335-0455-6

Library of Congress Cataloging-in-Publication Data

Storms, C. Samuel, 1951–
    To the one who conquers : 50 daily meditations on the seven letters of Revelation 2–3 /
Sam Storms.
       p. cm.
    Includes index.
    ISBN 978-1-4335-0138-8 (tpb)
    1. Bible. N.T. Revelation II-III—Meditations. 2. Jesus Christ. I. Title.

BS2825.54.S76 2008
242'.2—dc22
                           2008006384

VP   16 15 14 13 12 11 10 09 08
         9   8   7   6   5   4   3   2   1

To

Greg Beale

Seminary classmate,
Wheaton College colleague,
biblical scholar,
student of Revelation,
and most important of all,
cherished and beloved friend

Contents

Contents

An Introduction to the Seven Letters to the Seven Churches

Aside from the occasional handwritten "thank you" note, I honestly can't remember the last time I received a personal letter from a personal friend. With the availability of the computer, the Internet, and of course, e-mail, rarely does anyone bother to write an actual letter (with a greeting, proper grammar, and a salutation).

I miss it. My filing cabinet was formerly filled with bulky manila folders labeled "Correspondence." The last one is dated 1995. Now I receive text messages on my cell phone, daily e-mails by the dozen, and countless attachments. But no letters.

I started reflecting on this as I began my study of the seven letters that Jesus sent to the seven churches in Asia Minor. I'm sure it was a thrilling experience for churches like those in Thessalonica or Philippi to receive a letter from the apostle Paul. But to receive *a personal letter from Jesus himself*, addressed specifically to your congregation, must have been overwhelming to its recipients. Countless emotional responses were no doubt forthcoming, everything from unbridled joy to fearful anticipation to deep conviction for sin.

These seven letters that constitute the focus of this book of devotional studies have long been a source of curiosity and learning by Christians throughout the last nineteen hundred or so years. All too often, however, we've read them as if they were addressed exclusively to other Christians of a bygone age, containing criticism and counsel and encouragement that carry little relevance for us who live in an age when personal letters have fallen on such hard times.

My purpose in writing these fifty brief meditations is to bring these letters from the first century into the twenty-first in a way that demonstrates their enormous relevance and practicality for the church today. I hope that you will read and meditate on these studies in a way that the letters on which they comment will come alive as the very Word of God for his people in the present day.

Needless to say, each letter was uniquely tailored for the needs of the church to which it was addressed. But the refrain at the close of each ("He who has an ear, let him hear what the Spirit says to the churches") indicates that our Lord intended for all Christians, both then and now, to heed his counsel and to profit from his perspective on what our lives as believers and as his body should be.

The Purpose of the Seven Letters

Why did Jesus commission John the apostle to send these seven letters to these seven churches? What is the purpose for these missives to the early church? Several theories have been suggested.

The first theory insists that we not lose sight of the fact that these churches were *concrete historical entities* to which John was instructed to write. In other words, these letters reflect realistic, often urgent circumstances existent in these churches. Consequently, the primary application is to the respective congregations and the problems they faced in the last half of the first century. Our Lord's aim, therefore, was primarily *pastoral*. He longed to address the needs of his people and provide them with appealing incentives for perseverance in the face of political oppression and social ridicule.

Another theory suggests that these churches represent seven different *types* of *churches* (even seven different types of *Christians*) that may be found not only in the first century but in any period of church history. This view arose partially in an attempt to explain why *these* seven churches were chosen and not others. There were other churches in Asia of equal, if not greater, importance, such as Troas (Acts 20:5ff.), Colossae (Col. 1:2), and Hierapolis (Col. 4:13). George Ladd suggests that "John chose these seven churches with which he was well acquainted so that they might be representative of the church at large."[1] Ramsay contends that the Asian church had slowly developed in an organization of seven groups and that at the center of each stood one of the seven churches to which John writes.[2]

Others place great stress on the fact that there are but *seven* churches, not six or eight, addressed. They contend that John intentionally chose seven because the number represents completeness or perfection or totality. Hence these churches point to the totality of all local assemblies and to the body of Christ universal (this is borne out by the symbolic significance of the number seven in Revelation). Note also, as mentioned above, that at the conclusion of each letter there is a wider address "to [all] the churches." Thus "although each letter is addressed to the particular situation of a particular church, it is relevant for the needs of all 'seven' of the churches, and consequently for the universal church."[3]

It has been suggested by a number of (but not all) dispensational, pretribulational premillennialists that these seven churches were specifically chosen because they reflect in their own condition the circumstances and state of the church at large during the inter-advent age. In other words, while affirming the historical, first-century primacy of the seven letters, they see in them a *prophecy* of the progressive stages of church history from John's time to the end of the age. Walter Scott writes:

Ecclesiastical pretension and departure from first love characterized the close of the apostolic period—*Ephesus* (2:1–7). Next succeeded the martyr period, which brings us down to the close of the tenth and last persecution, under Diocletian—*Smyrna* (2:8–11). Decreasing spirituality and increasing worldliness went hand in hand from the accession of Constantine and his public patronage of Christianity on to the seventh century—*Pergamos* (2:12–17). The papal church, which is Satan's masterpiece on earth, is witnessed in the assumption of universal authority and cruel persecution of the saints of God. Its evil reign covers "the middle ages," the moral characteristics of which have been well termed "dark." Popery blights everything it touches—*Thyatira* (2:18–29). The Reformation was God's intervention in grace and power to cripple papal authority and introduce into Europe the light which for 300 years has been burning with more or less brilliancy. Protestantism with its divisions and deadness shows clearly enough how far short it comes of God's ideal of the Church and Christianity—*Sardis* (3:1–6). Another Reformation, equally the work of God, characterized the beginning of last century—*Philadelphia* (3:7–13). The present general state of the professing Church which is one of lukewarmness is the most hateful and nauseous of any yet described. We may well term the last phase of church history on the eve of judgment, the christless period—*Laodicea* (3:14–22). Note that the history of the first three centuries is consecutive; whereas

13

the history of the remaining four overlaps, and then practically runs concurrently to the end—the Coming of the Lord.[4]

This view obviously believes that the sequence in which the seven churches are addressed was chosen in order to provide a *prophetic foreshadowing* of subsequent church history. However, a simple glance at a map indicates that the sequence is based on these churches as centers of communication for an itinerant Christian messenger. In other words, "Ephesus was the messenger's natural place of entry to the mainland of the province of Asia, and the other cities lay in sequence on a circular route round its inner territories."[5] From Ephesus (which is a mere 60 miles from the island of Patmos), the courier would travel virtually due north to Smyrna, approximately 35 miles, then slightly northwest to Pergamos, about 50 miles. From there he would turn in a southeasterly direction to Thyatira, then to Sardis, then to Philadelphia, and finally to Laodicea. In sum, the churches are addressed in the precise sequence in which they would be visited by a courier or merchant.

The Place of the Letters in the Structure of the Book

One can't help but notice that the letters of chapters 2 and 3 stand in antithetical parallelism to Revelation 21 and 22. In other words, the *imperfections* of the church in the *old creation*, as seen in the seven letters, find their counterpart in the *perfections* of the church in the *new creation*, as seen in chapters 21 and 22. Consider these unmistakable parallels identified by Meredith Kline:

- false prophets (2:2) / twelve true apostles (21:14);
- false Jews (2:9; 3:9) / the names of the tribes of true Israel (21:12);
- Christians dwell where Satan's throne is (2:13) / Christians dwell where God's throne is (22:1);
- some in the church are dead (3:1) / all in the new Jerusalem are written in the Lamb's book of life (21:27);
- the church is a faltering, temporal lampstand (1:20; 2:5) / God and the Lamb are the eternal lamps (21:23–24; 22:5);
- the church is filled with idolatrous impurities (2:14–15, 20) and liars (2:9; 3:9) / there will be only purity and truth in the new creation (21:8, 27).

- Christians face persecution, hoping in God's promises to over-comers (2:8–10, 14) / in the new creation they reign, having inherited these promises.[6]

Similarly, Paul Minear[7] has noted that each of the promises made to the "overcomers" or "conquerors" is perfectly fulfilled in the final vision of the consummated new creation:

- food (2:7 and 22:2);
- the temple (3:12 and 21:22ff.);
- identification with an eternal city (3:12 and 21:2,10);
- a great name (3:12 and 22:4);
- eternal security (3:5 and 21:27);
- incorruptible clothing (3:5 and 21:2, 9ff.; cf. 19:7–8);
- a bright stone and a luminary (2:17, 28, and 21:11, 18–21, 23; 22:5, 16);
- a share in Christ's kingly power (2:26–27; 3:21 and 22:5);
- exclusion from the second death (2:11 and 21:7–8).

The Literary Structure of the Letters

There appears to be a standard structure to the letters, with a few exceptions noted below. Each letter can be divided into seven sections:

(1) a command to write to an angel of the church;
(2) a self-description by Jesus derived from the vision of chapter 1, introduced by the formula, "these things";
(3) commendation of the church's good works;
(4) an accusation of some sin;
(5) an exhortation to repent with either a warning of judgment or a word of encouragement;
(6) an exhortation to discern the truth of the preceding message ("he who has an ear . . .");
(7) a promise to the overcomers.

Beale notes the slight alterations from this pattern: "The third section is lacking in the letter to Laodicea. The fourth and second parts of the fifth are lacking in the letters to Smyrna and Philadelphia, since those churches are regarded as faithful."[8]

We should also note that the seven churches seem to fall into three groups. Group one would be the first and seventh, both of which are in danger of losing their identity as a Christian congregation. The second and sixth letters are written to churches that have proved themselves faithful and loyal to Christ's name. The three central letters (third, fourth, and fifth) have, to varying degrees, some people who have remained faithful and others who have not. Beale suggests that in light of this we should see the churches presented in the literary form of a chiasm:

A (first letter)
    B (second letter)
        C (third letter)
        C (fourth letter)
        C (fifth letter)
    B' (sixth letter)
A' (seventh letter)

The significance of this, notes Beale,

> is that the Christian church *as a whole* is perceived as being in poor condition, since not only are the healthy churches in a minority but the literary pattern points to this emphasis because the churches in the worst condition form the literary boundaries of the letters and the churches with serious problems form the very core of the presentation. This is highlighted as we recognize that at the center of the middle letter stands a general statement that "all the churches will know" that Christ is the omniscient judge of his unfaithful followers (2:23). This statement is conspicuous as the only thing said in the letters about all "churches" other than at the conclusion of each letter.[9]

All these factors add to the mystery and beauty of our Lord's very personal and always very pointed assessment of the state of the local church. Once we have taken into consideration the original historical setting of each church and the factors unique to each, there are numerous lessons of immense importance for us today that we ignore to our peril.

The Jesus-driven Church

One cannot read these seven letters without noting the utter and unequivocal *Christocentricity* of their content. Jesus is the center of which all church life is the circumference. He is the head of the church, both local and universal. He is the unrivaled Lord over all. He is himself the standard according to which the life of every congregation is judged and the One whose person and personality shape the beliefs and behavior of all. He is the one who walks among the lampstands (i.e., the churches; 2:1) and exercises exclusive sovereignty over the life of every congregation. He knows their works, their trials and tribulation, and the circumstances where they dwell. Indeed, nothing escapes his all-penetrating gaze. The condition of each church is an open book before him. He reads every heart, evaluates every motive, assesses every work, and will bring every person into judgment according to the deeds each has performed.

The spiritual condition of each body of believers is only as good as their faithful adherence to what Jesus has taught them and their perseverance in bearing witness to him in the face of persecution. Quite simply, if a church is not Jesus-driven, it stands on the brink of certain discipline (cf. 2:5; 2:16; 3:3; 3:19). The only thing that ultimately matters is the degree to which a church corporately and the lives of its members individually are shaped and fashioned according to the likeness of him who is Lord indeed.

In the final analysis, Jesus cares comparatively little about numerical size, cultural relevance, social influence, or financial prosperity. What matters most to him and must therefore matter most to us is whether a church holds forth *his* name, proclaims the gospel of which *he* is the center, and heeds *his* words as guidance to govern its life and loves. Is your church Jesus-driven? Are the ministries and programs of your corporate existence energized and given shape by what pleases him? Is he prized above all earthly treasures? Is faithfulness unto death an easy choice for you and those of your congregation?

I can only hope and most assuredly pray, as you read and ponder these meditations, that God would apply the salve of his Spirit to your eyes that you might see the beauty of his Son in this glorious revelation within the Revelation!

Sam Storms

Part 1

The Church in Ephesus

To the angel of the church in Ephesus write: "The words of him who holds the seven stars in his right hand, who walks among the seven golden lampstands. I know your works, your toil and your patient endurance, and how you cannot bear with those who are evil, but have tested those who call themselves apostles and are not, and found them to be false. I know you are enduring patiently and bearing up for my name's sake, and you have not grown weary. But I have this against you, that you have abandoned the love you had at first. Remember therefore from where you have fallen; repent, and do the works you did at first. If not, I will come to you and remove your lampstand from its place, unless you repent. Yet this you have: you hate the works of the Nicolaitans, which I also hate. He who has an ear, let him hear what the Spirit says to the churches. To the one who conquers I will grant to eat of the tree of life, which is in the paradise of God."

1

Does Your Church Have an Angel?

Revelation 2:1

"To the angel of the church in Ephesus write: 'The words of him who holds the seven stars in his right hand, who walks among the seven golden lampstands.'"

No," said one person in response to the question in the title above. "But we've got plenty of demons!"

Hmmm. I'm not sure what to say to that. But let's get back to the original question. It's not entirely without warrant, for each of the seven letters to the seven churches in Asia Minor is addressed to an "angel" (see Rev. 2:1, 8, 12, 18; 3:1, 7, 14). What could Jesus possibly have meant when he instructed John to send this letter "to the angel of the church in Ephesus"?

There have been countless theories about the identity of these angels, none of which is entirely satisfying to me. But let's take a brief look at the more popular suggestions.

1) When I was still an active member of a Southern Baptist church, I heard my pastor (who will remain unnamed) argue that the "angel" in each case was the senior pastor of the congregation! This isn't to say that all Southern Baptist pastors see themselves in this text, but it is a view that warrants comment. There are several reasons why I find this theory unlikely.

First, it is contrary to the New Testament portrait of church structure. Nowhere in the New Testament is a single individual described as exercising pastoral authority over a congregation. Rule by a *plurality of elders* is the standard biblical perspective. To argue otherwise is to assume, falsely, in my opinion, that there was an evolutionary development in biblical ecclesiology in which a plurality of leadership in the early years of the church's existence gradually gave way to a singular pastoral authority. In terms of *historical* development, subsequent to the closing of the biblical canon, this is precisely what happened (the first indication of a single pastor or bishop is found in the writings of Ignatius [about A.D. 110] and Clement of Rome). But that is far removed from saying it occurred within the canon itself.

Second, the word *angel* is used some sixty times in Revelation and always means a supernatural or spiritual being. This is not a decisive objection, but it does place the burden of proof on the one who contends that the word here deviates from its standard use in the Apocalypse.

Third, the word *angel* is used nowhere else in the New Testament to designate an ecclesiastical office. Again, that doesn't mean it can't be applied that way in the seven letters, but it would be unique in the biblical revelation if it were.

Fourth, and finally, we know from Acts 20:17–38 that the Ephesian church was ruled by a plurality of elders. So, although I do believe in the legitimacy of a "senior" or "lead" pastor of a congregation (although he remains one elder among a plurality who govern the body), I seriously doubt this is what Jesus had in mind when he used the word *angel* in these seven letters.

2) Another possibility is that the "angel" refers to a prophet or delegated representative of the church. This person may have functioned in an ambassadorial role, or perhaps as somewhat of a secretary who was responsible for maintaining communication with those outside the congregation as well as other tasks that may have been assigned. On this view stress is placed on the literal meaning of the Greek term *angelos*, which means messenger (cf. Luke 9:52; James 2:25).

3) Yet a third, more likely option, points to the fact that in Revelation 1:11 (cf. 1:4) the letters are directed to "the churches" (plu-

ral). So also at the end of each letter we read: "Let him hear what the Spirit says to the *churches*." Thus the Lord speaks to the *whole church* and not just to an "angel." This leads some to conclude that the angel *is* the church, i.e., a personification of the church. The Greek text would certainly allow (but by no means require) this interpretation, in which case we would translate: "to the angel *which is* the church in Ephesus."

Needless to say, this view suffers from the same weakness as the first two options in that it requires that we deviate from the regular use of the term *angel* in the book of Revelation (where it refers to a supernatural, nonhuman, being). There is also the fact that in Revelation 1:20 the angels of the seven churches are described as distinct from the seven churches themselves, making their identification less likely.

4) Another theory is that the "angel" of each church is its guardian angel. Although some scoff at the notion of angels providing this kind of service or ministry to the body of Christ, we should not dismiss it too quickly.

Angels are described as "ministers" (*leitourgos*), a word that suggests a priestly service (Heb. 1:7, 14; cf. Ps. 103:19–21). They provide guidance and direction for God's people (Gen. 24:7, 40; Ex. 14:19; see also Ex. 23:20; Num. 20:16; Acts 5:17–20; 8:26; 10:3–7, 22; 16:9), as well as comfort and encouragement (Matt. 4:11; Luke 22:43; Acts 27:22–24). Angels also guard and protect the children of God, as is clear from Psalms 34:7; 78:23–25; 91:11; 1 Kings 19:5–7; and Daniel 6:20–23; 12:1.

Acts 12:15 is an unusual passage, in that we read of believers who mistook Peter himself for "his angel." It's possible that Luke is only describing their belief without himself endorsing it (but I find this unlikely). Others argue that he intends to teach that each of us not only has a guardian angel but also that the latter may assume our physical characteristics. Yes, it seems odd, but why else would they have concluded that the "person" at the door was Peter's angel and not someone or something else?

Matthew 18:10 is especially interesting. There Jesus warns against the neglect of little children and reminds his disciples that "their angels always see the face of my Father who is in heaven." An ancient custom prevailed in Eastern court settings according to which those who stood "before the king" or were allowed to "see his face" were officers who enjoyed the king's special favor and were privileged to enjoy the closest possible fellowship. The implication may be that *the highest ranking angels* are assigned and commissioned by God to watch over with loving care his "little ones." Thus Jesus is saying, "Don't despise my 'little ones,' for they are so highly regarded that God has appointed his most illustrious angels to keep watch over them."

Their continual presence before God, beholding his face, may mean one of two things: (1) it may be a way of saying that our condition and needs are ever before God; he is always and ever alert to our situation in life; or (2) their constant presence before him is for the purpose of quickly responding to whatever tasks God may assign them in their ministry to us. (One might be tempted to ask: If these angels "continually" stand before the face of God in heaven, how can they serve as daily or continual "guardians" of people on earth?)

The most basic and obvious problem with this view is that it doesn't make sense why Jesus would address the letter to the guardian angel of a church rather than directly to the congregation itself. What need would there be to do so, and what purpose would it serve? Perhaps a good answer for this is forthcoming. But at this point, I don't know what it would be.

As you can see, there is no definitive explanation for who these angels were or what function they discharged. If pressed to make a choice, I would opt for either the third or fourth interpretation. In any case, our responsibility to heed the counsel of Christ in each letter does not hang suspended on our ability to decipher the identity of the "angel" to whom each letter was sent.

2

Loving Jesus in Ephesus

Revelation 2:1

"**To the angel of the church in Ephesus write**: 'The words of him who holds the seven stars in his right hand, who walks among the seven golden lampstands.'"

There are times when I wonder if it can get any worse here in America. Recently a man barricaded himself in an Amish schoolhouse and proceeded to shoot eleven helpless young girls in the head. As of today, five are dead and the others linger in critical condition. A prominent legislator has been caught sending sexually explicit messages to a young page in our nation's capital. Idolatry is rampant. Sexual perversion is applauded. Jesus is mocked.

Don't misunderstand me. I love my country. I love my city. But how bad can it get? Well, actually, a lot worse! Some day it might even be as bad for us as it was for believers living in Ephesus in the latter years of the first century.

It's appropriate that the first of the seven letters was sent to Ephesus, for although not the titular capital of Asia (Pergamum held that honor), it was the most important political center of all. By the time the church received this letter, the city of Ephesus had grown to a population of about 250,000. By their standards, it was huge. It was, in effect, the New York City of the ancient world.

We *honor* our President and pray *for* him, and rightly we should (1 Pet. 2:17; 1 Tim. 2:1–2). But in Ephesus, *worship* of the Roman emperor was mandatory. Prayer *to* him was normative. Scattered across the landscape of America are presidential libraries, bearing the names and housing the historical artifacts of men such as Harry S. Truman, John F. Kennedy, Ronald Reagan, and Bill Clinton. Not so in Ephesus. There one would find, not libraries, but temples dedicated to the idolatrous veneration of such as Claudius, Hadrian, Julius Caesar, Augustus, and Severus. Every day Christian men and women in Ephesus passed these imposing structures, going about their daily tasks in an atmosphere filled with pagan praise of mere humans.

Worse still, religion and superstition were hopelessly intertwined, and the magical arts were widely prevalent (cf. Acts 19:19). Ephesus was a seething cauldron of countless cults and superstitions. Pre-eminent among all religious attractions was the Temple of Diana (Artemis), construction of which began in 356 B.C. It was regarded as one of the Seven Wonders of the Ancient World. The platform on which the temple was built measured more than 100,000 square feet. Its dimensions were 425 feet long, 220 feet wide (hence, 93,500 square feet), and 60 feet high. Some 127 pillars were of Parian marble and thirty-six were overlaid with gold and jewels.

Christianity came to Ephesus with Aquila and Priscilla in A.D. 52 when Paul left them there as he traveled from Corinth to Antioch (Acts 18:18–22). On his next missionary journey Paul remained and worked in Ephesus for more than two years (Acts 18:8, 10) and some time later Timothy ministered there (1 Tim. 1:3). The effect of the gospel in that city is best illustrated by the incident recorded in Acts 19:23–41 (especially vv. 23–29). The theater mentioned in that passage could accommodate more than twenty-four thousand people. I, like many others, have had the privilege of standing on its excavated ruins.

It was believed that the apostle John spent his final years in Ephesus, from which city he also wrote his Gospel account and where, according to Eusebius, he was buried. Later tradition also locates the grave of Mary, mother of Jesus, in Ephesus.

I suspect that many of you often wonder if it's possible for a Christian, indeed a church, to flourish in the cities of our nation. Here in Kansas City one finds the international headquarters for one of the largest Unitarian movements in our nation, as well as the center for the Reorganized Church of Latter Day Saints. There are Muslim and Buddhist shrines, together with schools and other facilities devoted to false religions of a wide variety. Yet, I can make it through most days without ever encountering such folk or feeling their presence. I never have to worry about persecution on Sunday morning or being threatened with confiscation of my property or imprisonment for failing to pay homage to any local or national political figure. If I were to be beaten or arrested for sharing my faith, there are laws in place to protect my rights and vindicate my name. Not so in Ephesus.

The first church to receive a letter from Jesus was located in a city that wasn't even remotely Christian. No laws existed to protect their freedom of religious expression. The worship of false deities was institutionalized. The only things on which the Ephesian believers could rely were God himself and one another. Yet, as we'll note in a subsequent lesson, they labored faithfully for the gospel, endured patiently, and were intolerant of evil. Yes, the church had its problems, for which Jesus issues a stern rebuke, but its members had not abandoned the faith.

How would you and I fare in such a pagan atmosphere? I ask this because it often appears to me that many Christians believe the church in America can survive only if it is afforded legislative protection, only if politically conservative and Christian candidates are elected to national and local office, only if the next appointee to the Supreme Court is pro-life, only if prayer is restored to our public schools.

Make no mistake: I'm eternally grateful for the laws that safeguard our rights, and I consistently vote for those candidates who are social, fiscal, and moral conservatives. But have we come so to depend on such political blessings, economic liberties, and the legal protection Christianity enjoys that in their absence we fear the destruction of the church and the silencing of our witness?

The church in Ephesus, as with so many other congregations in the first century, knew nothing of a constitution, a first amendment, or a right to vote. Yet they survived, and thrived, in the midst of what strikes us as unimaginable state-sanctioned idolatry and immorality. Before we panic or lose heart at the state of our state, or the condition of our city, we would do well to remember the promise of Jesus: "I will build my church, and the gates of hell shall not prevail against it" (Matt. 16:18).

3

Christ in and over His Church

Revelation 2:1

"To the angel of the church in Ephesus write: '**The words of him who holds the seven stars in his right hand, who walks among the seven golden lampstands.**'"

Several years ago John Stott wrote an excellent little book on the seven letters in Revelation 2–3 entitled, *What Christ Thinks of the Church*.[1] Sad to say, there are some today who purport to be either church-growth experts or skilled ecclesiastical analysts and/or consultants who honestly don't seem to care much about what Christ thinks of the church. Yes, that sounds a bit harsh on my part, but let me explain.

I've often lamented what I call the loss of the "functional" authority of Scripture in the body of Christ in our day. Most Christians are diligent to affirm that the Bible is the inspired Word of God, the only infallible rule for faith and practice. But you could never tell that from the way they actually structure their churches or formulate their beliefs or cast their vision or shepherd their sheep. In other words, there is a vast chasm separating their theological affirmation of what the Bible is, as God's Word, and how they employ the biblical text in shaping the strategy and expression of ministry. All too often, the Bible bears a token authority that rarely translates into a functional guide and governor, so to speak, that dictates and directs what we are to believe and how we are to be God's people in a postmodern world.

So, when I say that certain folk don't appear to care much about what Christ thinks of the church, I have in mind the way in which they elevate sociological trends and marketing surveys and demographic studies, together with the "felt needs" of the congregation, above the principles and truths of Scripture itself. That's not to say we can't learn from the former; only that an undue focus on them often leads to the neglect of Scripture and even the abandonment of clear biblical guidelines on how to "do church."

I feel considerable energy on this point because of what I see in Revelation 2:1. There we read, "To the angel of the church in Ephesus write: 'The words of him who holds the seven stars in his right hand, who walks among the seven golden lampstands.'"

Are you as moved as I am by the fact that these are the "words" of Christ himself (lit., "these things he says")? Yes, all Scripture is God-breathed (2 Tim. 3:16). Every statement in the Bible is the revelatory "word" of our great God and Savior. But these seven letters are the direct and explicit address of the risen Christ to his people. He addresses his church in "words": statements, assertions, propositional utterances, theological concepts, doctrinal truths, ethical demands, etc. We would do well to heed what he says!

But second, I want you to notice how Jesus is described. Earlier in Revelation 1:12ff. John is granted a vision of the glorified Christ. The significant thing is that each of the seven letters in chapters two and three begins with a description of our Lord taken from that remarkable vision. (Others have also argued that each description is uniquely appropriate to the situation of that particular church.)

The letter to the church in Ephesus proceeds from him who "holds" the seven stars in his right hand and who "walks" in the midst of the seven golden lampstands. The meaning of this symbolism is given in the immediately preceding verse (Rev. 1:20). When John turned he saw "seven golden lampstands," a clear allusion to Zechariah 4:2, 10. Most believe that the lampstand in Zechariah with its seven lamps symbolizes the temple and by extension the faithful within Israel. Here in Revelation the lampstands represent the church. The church is to serve as a light to the world. In the middle of these lampstands is the risen Christ. "Part of Christ's priestly role is to tend the lampstands. The Old Testament priest would trim the lamps, remove the wick and old oil, refill the lamps with fresh oil, and relight those that had gone out. Likewise, Christ tends the ecclesial lampstands by commending, correcting, exhorting, and warning . . . in order to secure the churches' fitness for service as lightbearers in a dark world."[2]

What is of special note to us is the *advance* made from the description in 1:13, 16 to that of 2:1. Jesus not only "has" the stars, he "holds" (lit., grasps) them. He not only "stands" in the midst of the lampstands, he "walks" among them! The lordship of Christ over his people is not passive, distant, or indifferent. It is active, immanent, and intimate. Our Lord patrols the churches with an intense and ever present awareness of all thoughts, deeds, and activities. Thus it is no surprise that each letter contains the ominous, "I know your works" (2:2, 9, 13, 19; 3:1, 8, 15).

The move from "has" to "holds" and from "stands" to "walks" is designed to highlight both the sovereignty of Christ over the church and his loving presence and unfailing ministry within it.

He "holds" or "grasps" the church because it belongs to him. He owns it. He has redeemed it by his blood. At no time does the church slip from his grasp or elude his grip or operate under its own authority. As difficult as church life often becomes, Christ never ceases to be its Sovereign. As disillusioning as human behavior within the church can be, it ever remains "his" body.

But more important still is the fact that he "walks" among the lampstands. He is present in and among his people. He guards and protects and preserves the church. He is never, ever absent! No service is conducted at which he fails to show up. No meal is served for which he does not sit down. No sermon is preached that he does not evaluate. No sin is committed of which he is unaware. No individual enters an auditorium of whom he fails to take notice. No tear is shed that escapes his eye. No pain is felt that his heart does not share. No decision is made that he does not judge. No song is sung that he does not hear.

How dare we build our programs and prepare our messages and hire our staffs and discipline our members as if he were distant or unaware of every thought, impulse, word, or decision! How dare we cast a vision or write a doctrinal statement or organize a worship service as if the Lord whose church it is were indifferent to it all!

Do you care what Christ thinks of the church? Or are you more attuned to the latest trend in worship, the most innovative strategy for growth, the most "relevant" way in which to engage the surrounding culture? Yes, Jesus cares deeply about worship. Of course he wants the church to grow. And he longs to see the culture redeemed for his own glory. All the more reason to pray that God might quicken us to read and heed the "words" of Christ to the church in Ephesus then and to the church now, whatever its name, denomination, or size. It obviously matters to him. Ought it not to us as well?

4

Our Knowledge
of God's Knowledge of Us

Revelation 2:2a

"**I know your works**, your toil and your patient endurance, and how you cannot bear with those who are evil, but have tested those who call themselves apostles and are not, and found them to be false.'"

Sin is strengthened by the illusion of secrecy. The wicked justifies his iniquity by saying "in his heart, 'God has forgotten, he has hidden his face, he will never see it'" (Psalm 10:11). Believing that his thoughts are known only to himself, he covets. Convinced that his fantasies are private affairs, he lusts. Persuaded that no one has access to his heart, he hates and blasphemes and revels in the passions of his flesh. Confident that God is either unable or unwilling to take note of his deeds, he steals, murders, fornicates, and lies.

But Jesus shatters the fantasy, both for Christian and non-Christian, by declaring: "I know your works!" Indeed, this riveting claim appears at the beginning of each of the seven letters. In five of those instances the same refrain is found: "I know your works" (cf. Rev. 2:2, 13, 19; 3:1, 8, 15). In the seventh (Rev. 2:9), he proclaims, "I know your tribulation and your poverty."

How does *your knowledge of God's knowledge of you* change your life? If it doesn't, it should. Consider these affirmations of the knowledge that God has of your soul. It is both pervasive and perfect.

"And you, Solomon my son, know the God of your father and serve him with a whole heart and with a willing mind, for the LORD searches all hearts and understands every plan and thought." (1 Chron. 28:9a)

O God, you know my folly; the wrongs I have done are not hidden from you. (Ps. 69:5)

The eyes of the LORD are in every place, keeping watch on the evil and the good. (Prov. 15:3).

Sheol and Abaddon lie open before the LORD; how much more the hearts of the children of man! (Prov. 15:11)

Why do you say, O Jacob, and speak, O Israel, "My way is hidden from the LORD, and my right is disregarded by my God"? Have you not known? Have you not heard? The LORD is the everlasting God, the Creator of the ends of the earth. He does not faint or grow weary; his understanding is unsearchable. (Isa. 40:27–28)

The heart is deceitful above all things, and desperately sick; who can understand it? "I the LORD search the heart and test the mind, to give every man according to his ways, according to the fruit of his deeds." (Jer. 17:9–10; see also Jer. 16:17; 18:23; 1 Kings 8:39)

O LORD of hosts, who tests the righteous, who sees the heart and the mind . . . (Jer. 20:12)

And the Spirit of the LORD fell upon me, and he said to me, "Say, Thus says the LORD: So you think, O house of Israel. For I know the things that come into your mind." (Ezek. 11:5)

"For your Father knows what you need before you ask him." (Matt. 6:8)

And they prayed and said, "You, Lord, who know the hearts of all, show which one of these two you have chosen." (Acts 1:24)

No creature is hidden from his sight, but all are naked and exposed to the eyes of him to whom we must give account. (Heb. 4:13)

God is greater than our heart, and he knows everything. (1 John 3:20)

God's knowledge of the inner man is also affirmed in Deuteronomy 31:21; 1 Samuel 16:7; Psalm 94:9–11; Isaiah 66:18; Jeremiah 11:20; 32:19; Luke 16:15 ("God knows your hearts"); Acts 15:8; Rom. 8:27 ("he who searches hearts"); 1 Corinthians 3:20; 1 Thessalonians 2:4; and Revelation 2:23. For his awareness of all our activities and ways, see also 1 Samuel 2:3; Job 23:10; 24:23; 31:4; Psalms 1:6; 33:13–15; 37:18; 119:168; Isaiah 29:15; and Matthew 10:30.

Let's think for a moment about how God thinks! The first thing to remember is that whereas we *learn* by observation and reason—we employ induction and deduction—God simply *knows*. His knowledge is intuitive, innate, and immediate. He neither discovers nor forgets.

More than that, he knows everything at once. With God, the act of knowing is complete and instantaneous. He thinks about all things at the same time, and is never not thinking about them (forgive the double negative!). As Wayne Grudem said, if God "should wish to tell us the number of grains of sand on the seashore or the number of stars in the sky, he would not have to count them all quickly like some kind of giant computer, nor would he have to call the number to mind because it was something he had not thought about for a time. Rather, he knows all things at once. All of these facts and all other things that he knows are always fully present in his consciousness."[3]

God's knowledge of us and all things is independent; that is to say, he doesn't get it from anyone or anything external to himself. This was Isaiah's point in asking rhetorically, "Who has measured the Spirit of the LORD, or what man shows him his counsel? Whom did he consult, and who made him understand? Who taught him the path of justice, and taught him knowledge, and showed him the way of understanding?" (Isa. 40:13–14).

God's knowledge of you and me is both exhaustive and infallible. He knows everything and he knows it perfectly. He holds no false beliefs about us and makes no errors of judgment. God knows exhaustively all his own deeds and plans (Acts 15:18) as well as ours. No secret of the human heart, no thought of the mind or feeling of the soul escapes his gaze. Carl Henry points out, "Psychologists and psychoanalysts speak of deep areas of subconscious experience of which human beings are hardly aware. But God knows all men thoroughgoingly, psychologists and psychoanalysts and theologians included."[4] This is explicitly affirmed in Psalm 139:

> O LORD, you have searched me and known me! You know when I sit down and when I rise up; you discern my thoughts from afar. You search out my path and my lying down and are acquainted with all my ways. Even before a word is on my tongue, behold, O LORD, you know it altogether. (vv. 1–4)

"Searching" is an anthropomorphic image, for "God knows all things naturally and as a matter of course, and not by any effort on his part. Searching ordinarily implies a measure of ignorance which is removed by observation; of course this is not the case with the Lord; but the meaning of the Psalmist is, that the Lord knows us thoroughly as if he had examined us minutely, and had pried into the most secret corners of our being."[5]

David's choice of words is designed to encompass the totality of his life's activities. God's knowledge extends to every posture, gesture, exercise, pursuit, state, and condition possible. When I am active and when I am passive and everything in between, you know it all! My most common and casual acts, my most needful and trivial moments—none escapes your eye!

Every emotion, feeling, idea, thought, conception, resolve, aim, doubt, motive, perplexity, and anxious moment lies before God like an open book. And God knows all this "from afar"! The distance between heaven and earth by which men vainly imagine God's knowledge to be circumscribed (limited, bounded) offers no obstacle. Spurgeon said it best:

> Though my thought be invisible to the sight, though as yet I be not myself cognizant of the shape it is assuming, yet thou hast it under thy consideration, and thou perceivest its nature, its source, its drift, its result. Never dost thou misjudge or wrongly interpret me; my inmost thought is perfectly understood by thine impartial mind. Though thou shouldest give but a glance at my heart, and see me as one sees a passing meteor moving afar, yet thou wouldst by that glimpse sum up all the meanings of my soul, so transparent is everything to thy piercing glance.[6]

God knows "all my ways," which is to say that every step, every move, every journey, is under his gaze. What possible hope of concealment is there when God knows before we do what we will say? Before we utter a word, God knows it all (thoroughly, completely, accurately; v. 4).

So, if sin is strengthened by the illusion of secrecy, what better way to destroy its power than by meditating on the exhaustive and gloriously infallible knowledge that God has of us! Here again is the declaration of Jesus: "I know your works."

5

When God Crowns
His Own Grace

Revelation 2:2a

"I know your works, your toil and your patient endurance, and
how you cannot bear with those who are evil, but have tested
those who call themselves apostles and are not, and found them
to be false."

In the previous meditation, we saw how sin is strengthened by
the illusion of secrecy. Some people are emboldened in iniquity on the false assumption that God is either unaware of or
indifferent to their deeds. Countering this are the numerous texts
we noted that affirm the knowledge God has of our most intimate
intentions and activities. To these, Jesus also adds: "I know your
works" (Rev. 2:2a).

Knowing that the Lord knows is not simply a reason to desist
from sin. For the Christian it's an encouragement and incentive for
perseverance in faithfulness and obedience. How often have you or
has someone you know felt discouraged, disconsolate, tempted to
throw in the towel because you were convinced that no one, not
even God, knew or cared about your diligence and sincere efforts
to serve the body of Christ?

Don't think for a moment this isn't an important issue. Consider how the author of Hebrews encouraged his readers with this
reminder: "For God is not unjust so as to overlook your work and

the love that you have shown for his name in serving the saints, as you still do" (6:10). As far as God is concerned, it's a matter of *divine justice* that he take note of your "work" and "love" in "serving the saints." To overlook or ignore your labors or act as if they were inconsequential is inconceivable to God!

But why? And why would it be a matter of *injustice* were he to overlook them? Be assured of this: you do not put God in your debt by your serving the saints. The appeal to justice does not mean God is obligated to acknowledge the worth of your works. Rather, our work in serving one another is done, as the text from Hebrews indicates, "for his sake" or more literally, "unto his name"! John Piper put it this way:

> What obliges the justice of God to remember our love is not the worth of our service, but the worth of his name. When we serve and work out of love for that name, what we are calling attention to is the worth of his name. This is why the justice of God is at stake in remembering our work and love. . . .When we serve the saints as a way of loving the name of God, God's justice commits him to remember our work and reward us for his name's sake (cf. Psalm 143:11; Hebrews 10:35; 11:26).[7]

All the works of the Ephesian believers, and ours too, if done in God's grace and for God's glory will never escape God's gaze. He sees and acknowledges and enjoys our "works" because they testify to his presence in our lives and his power in equipping us to do what is pleasing to him (cf. Heb. 13:20–21).

Remember Paul's words in Romans 15:18: "For I will not venture to speak of anything except what Christ has accomplished through me." Justice requires that God not overlook our works because *justice requires that God honor God*. We work only because God is working in and through us for his good will (Phil. 2:12–13). That is why, as it has often been said, when God rewards us for our works he will be crowning his own grace.

When our work is done in the name of Jesus, by means of the power of Jesus, and for the sake of Jesus, we can rest assured that the justice of Jesus requires that he know and acknowledge and reward what he has accomplished through us.

That is why Jesus makes the point in his reminder to the Ephesian church: "I know your works, your toil and your patient endurance, and how you cannot bear with those who are evil" (Rev. 2:2a).

In a book (Revelation) written to strengthen faith, the emphasis on works or deeds is important. Works are the criterion of the genuineness of faith. Whoever has true faith *works*. Whoever does not has not. With that understood, note carefully what Jesus says about their works.

His commendation of the church in Ephesus involves three virtues (cf. 1 Thess. 1:3). Under the general category of *works* or *deeds* we find the first two virtues identified as "toil" and "patient endurance." We'll take up the third virtue in the next meditation.

The word translated "toil" looks to something beyond routine effort and focuses on exertion to the point of exhaustion. It refers to a spending of oneself in arduous labor. Apparently Ephesus was a busy, active church. It no doubt had all the programs and activities we normally associate with a church that is spiritual and passionate. They were truly diligent and conscientious.

The translation "patient endurance" renders one word in the original text. The King James Version translates it as "patience" and the New American Standard Bible has "perseverance." Jesus is perhaps referring to their diligence in bearing the persecution and hostility of an unbelieving society. Despite the temptations that assaulted them from every quarter, they stood unswerving and firm in their allegiance to Christ.

Therefore, to every faithful servant of Christ who has labored in virtual obscurity in the nursery, I say: "Jesus knows your works!" To every Sunday school teacher who spends hours each week in preparation, though only a handful show up early enough for class, I say: "Jesus knows your works!" To every diligent believer who stuffs the bulletin with inserts or cleans up in the kitchen after a potluck dinner or picks up trash following the Sunday service, I say: "Jesus knows your works!"

Our Lord is ever mindful of those deeds that are rarely seen and perhaps never acknowledged by other humans. That visit to the nursing home to pray for a lonely widow was for an audience of One. That hot meal prepared for an ailing friend was a fragrant aroma to God. The Lord Jesus may often be the only one who knows, but it is enough that he knows. And I remind you again, he most assuredly knows!

But to each and all of these I also say, "Why do you work? Is it for perks and praise? Is it in hope that your name will be mentioned from the pulpit? Or is your labor and toil and patient endurance pursued for the sake of his name? Is your commitment to the saints and your service for the kingdom motivated by your love for God?" I pray that it is.

Take heart! Be encouraged! Be strengthened for ever greater and more persistent effort "unto God's name" and on behalf of his people, because "Jesus knows your works!"

6

The Limits of Love

Revelation 2:2, 6

"**I know** your works, your toil and your patient endurance, and **how you cannot bear with those who are evil, but have tested those who call themselves apostles and are not, and found them to be false. . . .** Yet this you have: you hate the works of the Nicolaitans, which I also hate."

Does love have its limits? Are there places it won't go, people it won't embrace, ideas it won't endorse? Or is true love indiscriminate, universal, and all-inclusive? These questions are clearly and decisively answered in our Lord's words to the church in ancient Ephesus. And his perspective is anything but politically correct!

Jesus had already commended the Ephesians for their hard work and perseverance. He now turns his attention to their orthodoxy. Far from being blinded by love, they had 20/20 discernment. They hated evil—period. No ifs, ands, or buts. Whatever form evil took, whether ethical or theological, they stood resolute in their opposition. No compromise. No cutting of corners. *Their love was revealed in their intolerance.* Unsanctified mercy had no place in the church at Ephesus. We would do well to learn from their example.

This virtue (yes, it *is* a virtue) is described in verses 2 and 6. This was their most stellar achievement. No heretical concept could ever raise its ugly head in Ephesus without being decapitated by

41

the swift stroke of biblical truth. The orthodoxy of the Ephesian church manifested itself in three ways:

First, according to verse 2a, they refused to bear with men of evil inclination. They firmly resisted those whose lives were outwardly licentious. We're not talking here about a momentary lapse or an inadvertent sin, but hardened and unrepentant iniquity. Had there been an inkling of conviction, a mere whisper of repentance, I trust the Ephesians would have responded with encouragement and exhortation and partnered with these people to bring them to faith in Jesus.

Second, according to verse 2b, they have tried and tested those who lay claim to being apostles. "Evil" men and false "apostles" is a twofold reference to the same group of individuals, the former a description of their disposition and the latter of their doctrine. The precise identity of these men is left unstated, but they were probably claiming to be part of the outer circle of apostles, beyond the twelve, which included James, Silas, and Barnabas (see Acts 14:14; 1 Cor. 15:7; Gal. 1:19; 1 Thess. 2:6).

Paul had warned the Ephesian elders of precisely this scenario. Upon returning to Palestine after the third missionary journey, Paul's ship put in at Miletus some thirty-five miles from Ephesus. He sent for the elders and spoke to them of the emergence within their midst of heretical teachers (see Acts 20:28–31). How did they respond? They listened . . . and they tested the spirits (1 John 4:1–6). For them, *heresy detected was heresy denied.* As Jesus said, they refused to "bear" with such men.

But note well: they rejected them only after "testing" them. This was no knee-jerk reaction. Yes, the Ephesians were strict, but they were fair. They listened, they studied, and above all, like the Bereans (cf. Acts 17:11), they tested the teaching of these men and weighed their claims on the scales of Scripture.

Third, according to verse 6, they joined Jesus in hating the deeds of the Nicolaitans (yes, Jesus does *hate* certain things, and so should we). Who were the Nicolaitans? Early tradition among the church fathers, most notably Irenaeus, identifies them with Nicolas, the proselyte of Antioch who was appointed one of the first seven deacons, or servants, in Acts 6:5. This, however, is highly unlikely.

They are mentioned again in 2:15 in the letter to Pergamum and by implication in 2:14 and 2:20–21. The name itself may be derived from two words that mean "victory" (*nikos*) and "people" (*laos*), thus the idea of their consumption or overpowering of the people. They were evidently licentious and antinomian and advocated an unhealthy compromise with pagan society and the idolatrous culture of Ephesus.

The "teaching" of the Nicolaitans should probably be identified with the "teaching" of Balaam (2:14–15). The similarity of language also suggests that Jezebel and her followers (2:20–24) constituted a group of Nicolaitans in Thyatira. They are all said to be guilty of enticing God's people to "eat food sacrificed to idols" and "practice immorality" (2:14–15, 20). In Revelation, to "fornicate" (*porneuo*) and its cognates usually are metaphorical for spiritual apostasy and idol worship (14:8; 17:1, 2, 4, 5, 15, 16; 18:3, 9; 19:2). When these words are used literally, they are part of vice lists (9:21; 21:8; 22:15).

The Ephesian believers, however, were not duped. Nor were they so naïve as to believe that Christian charity can tolerate such false teaching. Note also the contrast: they "bear" trials and tribulations for Christ's sake (v. 3), but they cannot "bear" the company of these evil men (vv. 2, 6). They endure persecution but not perversion.

There are many lessons here, but one in particular stands out: *Jesus hates moral and theological compromise.* Any appeal to grace to justify sin is repugnant to our Lord. Any attempt to rationalize immorality by citing the "liberty" we have in Christ is abhorrent to him and must be to us. True Christian love is never expressed by the tolerance of wickedness, whether it be a matter of what one believes or how one behaves.

Much is being said today about the extent of the church's engagement with culture. To what degree should we be involved? How narrowly should we draw the boundary lines for what is permissible, on the one hand, and what is off limits, on the other? There are no easy answers, but of one thing I'm sure. If "cultural relevancy" threatens in any way or degree to undermine your single-minded, wholehearted devotion to Christ, end it. To the extent that being "in" the world drains you of the necessary strength to resist its temptations or diminishes the purity of your relationship with Christ, turn and walk away.

Don't expect me or anyone else to identify on your behalf those activities or ideas or events or persons from which or from whom you should withdraw. If they are not explicitly noted in Scripture, or cannot be deduced by good and necessary reason, to legislate for others what is and is not permissible would be legalism. I can only make that decision for myself.

May God grant us the discernment to identify the "Nicolaitans" of our day and the moral conviction and *love* to be intolerant of their destructive doctrines.

7

For His Name's Sake

Revelation 2:3

"I know you are enduring patiently and bearing up for my name's sake, and you have not grown weary."

People patiently endure pain for any number of reasons. The world is filled with courageous men and women who suffer almost indescribable persecution and oppression. Prisons are filled not only with those properly convicted of a crime but also with people who refused to compromise or recant their philosophical convictions.

On any particular day you can turn on the TV or pick up a newspaper and read of yet someone else who was martyred for his political beliefs or subjected to substantial material and personal loss in the pursuit of social justice. Others persevere for profit or to generate compassion or pity or for any number of other reasons unrelated to the promotion and praise of the name of Christ.

But for the Christian, endurance is motivated by a singular passion. Perseverance is never an end in itself. Suffering for suffering's sake is silly. Worse still, it may be the sign of mental illness! No one likes pain, or at least no one should. There is no intrinsic value in the experience of discomfort or of being put upon or of suffering inconvenience. Even in the case of Jesus, it was "for the *joy* . . . set before him [that he] endured the cross, despising the shame" (Heb. 12:2). There was a goal for the sake of which he embraced the horror of Gethsemane and Calvary.

We also are called to take up our cross daily, although not for the purpose for which Jesus was nailed to one. We also are subjected to slander and humiliation and mocking laughter and disdain. So why persevere? Why not simply cut our losses and run? What's wrong, after all, with looking out for ourselves and preserving our health and welfare? Is there anything really worth patiently enduring undeserved attack and opposition?

Evidently the Ephesians thought so. I'm sure they were sorely tempted to deny Christ, to soften the word of their testimony. Money and physical comfort and the joy of simply being left alone can be a powerful and appealing temptation. But the Ephesians refused to budge. They yielded not an inch. "I know you are enduring patiently," said Jesus, "and bearing up for my name's sake, and you have not grown weary" (Rev. 2:3).

Let's be clear about their motivation, the goal in view of which they bore up under oppressive conditions: *it was for the sake of Christ's name*. That is to say, they endured with a view to making known, especially to their persecutors, that Jesus was a treasure of far greater worth than whatever physical or financial comfort their denial of him might bring.

We see the same perspective embraced by those described in Hebrews 10:34. They "joyfully accepted the plundering" of their "property," because they knew they "had a better possession and an abiding one." Or again, in Hebrews 11:24–26 we read of Moses turning his back on the royal perks of being called the son of Pharaoh's daughter, "choosing rather to be mistreated with the people of God than to enjoy the fleeting pleasures of sin." Why? What could possibly justify what appears to be such a foolish, costly, and painful decision? Answer: "He considered the reproach of Christ greater wealth than the treasures of Egypt, for he was looking to the reward" (v. 26).

This same passion, to see and savor Jesus alone, accounted for Paul's unqualified and otherwise inexplicable decision to turn his back on earthly achievements: "Whatever gain I had," said Paul, "I counted as loss *for the sake of Christ*. Indeed, I count everything as loss because of the surpassing worth of knowing Christ Jesus my Lord. *For his sake* I have suffered the loss of all things and count them as rubbish, in order that I may gain Christ and be found in him, not having a righteousness of my own that comes from the law, but that which comes through faith in Christ, the righteousness from God that depends on faith" (Phil. 3:7–9). Did you see it? It was for his sake, as it also was for the Ephesians.

In the case of the Ephesians, undoubtedly some suffered unto death while others experienced the blessing of deliverance. In both instances it was "for his name's sake." In dying, some declared, "Jesus is more precious than what I'm losing." In living, others declared, "Jesus is more precious than what I'm gaining." In both cases, Jesus is treasured above everything and thus magnified above all.

The sort of patient endurance that Jesus praises doesn't come easily. Our flesh screams to quit, to yield to the pressure, to capitulate to the alluring promise of worldly promotion and prestige. Relief is often only a word or two away. Money, comfort, and power are so readily within our grasp.

How can we strengthen *our* spirits so as not to "grow weary" (Rev. 2:3)? By what manner and means can we resist the temptation to compromise? Paul spoke directly to this point in Romans 15:4–5. The "God of endurance and encouragement" (v. 5), that is, the God from whom alone endurance and encouragement ultimately flow, supplies us with strength *through the Scriptures*. It is "through endurance and through the encouragement of the Scriptures" that we find hope and help to persevere (v. 4).

Enduring patiently and bearing up for the sake of Christ's name (Rev. 2:3) is made possible when we "see" his beauty in the revealed Word, when we are quickened by the Spirit to behold his majesty and to relish his glory and grace in the inspired testimony of the biblical text.

Will you then pray with me, "'Open my eyes,' O God, 'that I may behold wondrous things out of your law'" (Psalm 119:18)? "Help me to see Jesus in your Word. Unveil to the eyes of my heart the splendor of the King" (see Eph. 1:15ff.). "Build into my soul, through the knowledge of the surpassing excellency of Jesus my Lord, the power to persevere. Amen."

8

When Doctrine Isn't Enough

Revelation 2:4–5

"I have this against you, that you have abandoned the love you had at first. Remember therefore from where you have fallen; repent, and do the works you did at first. If not, I will come to you and remove your lampstand from its place, unless you repent.'"

There's never an excuse for bad theology. We must continually strive to refine our thoughts and bring them into ever increasing conformity to God's Word. But there comes a time when doctrine isn't enough.

Stop! Before we go forward with another word, please do not draw unwarranted conclusions from that statement. Don't think for a moment that simply because there is *more* to being a Christian than right thinking, being a Christian is possible with *less* than right thinking. When I say there comes a time when doctrine isn't enough, that in no way justifies theological laxity, compromise, or the embracing of anti-intellectualism, as if the mind did not matter.

What I'm saying is that Christianity necessarily entails *both* orthodox belief *and* obedient behavior. It's inconceivable to me that anyone would suggest that it only matters what we believe or, conversely, that it only matters how we behave. The two are inseparably wedded in the purposes of God, and each withers in the absence of the other.

Having said that, and it was critically important that I say it, we can now proceed to observe that our Lord's notable commendation of the Ephesians is coupled with an equally incisive complaint: "But I have this against you, that you have abandoned the love you had at first" (Rev. 2:4).

There's no agreement among scholars of Revelation as to what "love" the Ephesians had "abandoned" (ESV) or "left" (NASB). The answer depends in part on how one understands and translates the word "first." Does it mean "first" in terms of time or chronology? That is the view embraced by the ESV; as they render it, "You have abandoned the love you had at first." The idea would be that this is a "love" they experienced immediately after their conversion and during the early days of their Christian life. Although the ESV rendering doesn't require it, the implication would be that the "love" they had abandoned was *brotherly* love, love for other Christians in the church.

Others argue that this love was "first" in the sense that it is the most important love that anyone can experience, that is to say, it is that *primary* love for the Lord Jesus Christ that comes before or takes precedence over all other loves in terms of value. This view is suggested by the NASB, which translates, "You have left your first love." Surely, if the emphasis is on the "love" that is of preeminent importance, the "love" that must be pursued above all other loves, it is love for Jesus himself.

In his epistle to the Ephesians, written some thirty years earlier, Paul mentioned the fervency of their love for one another (1:15–16) and concluded the letter with a blessing on those "who love our Lord Jesus Christ with love incorruptible" (6:24). But now, notes Grant Osborne, "they had lost the first flush of enthusiasm and excitement in their Christian life and had settled into a cold orthodoxy with more surface strength than depth. The second generation of the church had probably failed to maintain the fervor of the first."[8] But which "love" had they now lost: love for one another or love for Jesus or perhaps love for both?

There are two contextual clues that I believe indicate the reference is primarily, but not exclusively, to "brotherly" love. First, how can it be that they've abandoned their love for Christ if in the immediately preceding verse (v. 3) Christ himself commends them for enduring patiently for his name's sake? The latter words imply, if not require, the devotion and affection and love for Jesus that would inspire them to suffer for the sake of promoting and praising his name. If they didn't fervently love Jesus, they wouldn't have endured patiently for his name's sake. And if their endurance wasn't motivated by this affection, Jesus would hardly have commended them for it.

A second clue comes from what follows in verse 5. There, as a repentant antidote, so to speak, to their diminishing love, Jesus commands them to "do the works you did at first" (v. 5). This would more likely suggest that their lost love was love for one another that can be rekindled by deeds of kindness and compassion and self-sacrifice. See Romans 12:9–13 for an example of Christian brotherly love expressed in concrete deeds of service. This is especially made clear in 1 John 3:11–18 and 4:7–21.

On the other hand, I'm not certain we have to choose between the two. Jesus may well have had both "loves" in view. That the decrease in love for Christ issues in a loss of love for our fellow Christian is self-evident. Beasley-Murray put it this way:

> Where love for God wanes, love for man diminishes, and where love for man is soured, love for God degenerates into religious formalism, and both constitute a denial of the revelation of God in Christ. If the price paid by the Ephesians for the preservation of true Christianity was the loss of love, the price was too high, for Christianity without love is a perverted faith.[9]

In other words, I think Jesus could as easily have said to the Ephesians: "How dare you claim to love me at the same time you close your heart to a brother or sister in the body! And when you do love one another you demonstrate how much you love the One [i.e., me, Jesus] who gave himself for them" (see Heb. 6:10).

What we see in the church at Ephesus, therefore, was how their desire for orthodoxy and the exclusion of error had created a climate of suspicion and mistrust in which brotherly love could no longer flourish. Their eager pursuit of truth had to some degree soured their affections one for another. It's one thing not to "bear with those who are evil" (Rev. 2:2), but it's another thing altogether when that intolerance carries over to your relationship with other Christ-loving Christians!

Our Lord does not leave the Ephesians and their problem without a solution. Note the three terse commands of verse 5. Before doing so, however, observe what he does *not* recommend: he does not suggest that they become theologically lax, tolerant of error, or indifferent toward truth! In other words, don't try to cure one problem in a way that will create another.

So, then, here's his counsel. First, "*remember* . . . from where you have fallen" (v. 5a). Here their love is pictured as a height from which they had descended. To remember is to reflect and meditate on the peak of brotherly affection they once enjoyed. Recall the former fervor and let the memory of its joys and satisfaction stir you again to mutual devotion. Second, "*repent*" (v. 5b). Simply put, stop . . . then start. Stop the coldhearted disregard for one another—and for Jesus—and start cultivating that affection you formerly had. Third, "*do*." In particular, do "the works you did at first" (cf. Heb. 6:10).

How important is it that the Ephesians strive by God's grace to cultivate and sustain a passionate affection for both Christ and Christian? I'll let Jesus answer that question. If you don't repent, he solemnly warns, "I will come to you and remove your lampstand from its place" (Rev. 2:5).

What this means is that failure to comply will lead to the imminent termination of their influence or public witness (cf. 11:3–7, 10; see also Mark 4:21; Luke 8:16) as a body of believers. The "coming" of Jesus in verse 5 is not the second advent at the end of history but a "coming" in preliminary judgment and discipline of this church (cf. 2:16); the second advent, however, is probably in view in 2:25 and 3:11. It may even be that Jesus is threatening the end of this congregation's historical existence. I trust that such is enough to convince us all how important "love" is in the body of Christ!

Doctrinal precision is absolutely necessary. But it isn't enough. May God grant us grace to love others with no less fervor than we love the truth.

9

Feasting on the Tree of Life

Revelation 2:7

"He who has an ear, let him hear what the Spirit says to the churches. To the one who conquers I will grant to eat of the tree of life, which is in the paradise of God."

What comes to mind when I mention the word *heaven*? Streets of gold? Angelic choirs in adoration of the Lamb? The vindication of truth and justice? Yes, this and much more awaits the people of God. But the glory of heaven is primarily the presence of God. Heaven will be heavenly because God is there! All its beauty is a reflection of his glory; all blessings serve to enhance our enjoyment of him.

This is certainly true of the tree of life, mentioned here in Revelation 2:7 as a promise of Jesus to those who overcome: "He who has an ear, let him hear what the Spirit says to the churches. To the one who conquers I will grant to eat of the tree of life, which is in the paradise of God" (2:7). The tree of life is mentioned in three other texts as one of the features of the new heaven and new earth (see Rev. 22:2, 14, 19).

We must remember that the tree of life isn't an end in itself. We don't "conquer" or "overcome" (Rev. 2:7) simply to gain access to its fruit. The tree of life is a means to a higher and more exalted end, for it is good only so far as it sustains us to see and savor God. Its purpose is to nourish and support our eternal existence so that we might glorify God by enjoying him forever.

The appeal of the tree of life and what its preserving power brings us is cited by Jesus as an incentive to "conquer" or "overcome." Like the conclusion to each of the seven letters, this is an exhortation to heed what has been said. The exhortation assumes a mixed audience, not all of whom will respond positively (cf. Matt. 13:9–17; Mark 4:9, 23; Luke 8:8). When confronted with temptation or the pressure to abandon the faith, Jesus says loudly and clearly: *"Bring to mind the tree of life.* Meditate on its provision. For the one who conquers will eat of its blessed fruit forever!"

But surely something more is in mind than merely plucking fruit from an ordinary tree. There appear to be echoes here of the garden of Eden, reminding us that paradise future is the redemptive consummation of paradise past. Let me explain.

David Aune believes, and rightly so in my opinion, that the language of Revelation 2:7 points to "a restoration of God's original intention for humankind that was frustrated by sin, for Adam and Eve were expelled from the Garden of Eden to prevent them from eating of the tree of life (Gen. 3:24)."[10] Thus in paradise the verdict of Eden is reversed—"No longer will there be anything accursed" (Rev. 22:3). The original condition of Adam in his unfallen state will be restored and, no doubt, *enhanced,* as our righteousness will be eternal and irreversible. But Aune then goes on to suggest that "the tree of life is not simply a symbol for eternal life alone, but also represents the *cosmic center of reality* where eternal life is present and available, and where God dwells."[11]

There is something truly profound in the imagery found in verse 7 that may not be evident at first reading. This is where a knowledge of the cultural setting of the biblical text proves so rewarding. Colin Hemer contends that there was something analogous to the tree of life in the cult of Diana and the temple in Ephesus dedicated to her that makes this promise especially relevant.[12]

In the first place, the reference to the "tree" (*zulon*) of life may actually be an allusion to the cross of Christ. In the book of Acts (5:30; 10:39; 13:29) explicit reference is made to the "tree" (*zulon*) on which Jesus was crucified (likewise in Gal. 3:13 and 1 Pet. 2:24). By the way, the Greek word for "cross" (*stauros*) never occurs in Revelation.

Hemer also points to the fact that two passages in ancient literature describe the foundation of the Temple of Diana as a tree shrine. Inscriptions on coins from that era indicate that the tree, together with the bee and the stag, were distinctively associated with Diana of Ephesus. In addition, the temple was famous as a place of refuge or asylum for fleeing criminals. What makes this significant is that the word used to describe their experience is the same term used throughout the New Testament for our "salvation" (*soteria*).

The contrasts are both stunning and encouraging. For the Ephesian believers, "the cross [the tree of life] was the place of refuge for the repentant sinner in contrast with the tree [in Diana's temple] which marked the asylum for the unrepentant criminal."[13] Diana's so-called tree of refuge gave the criminal immunity and license to continue his life of rebellion and crime. Christ's tree of refuge, on the other hand, grants the repentant sinner eternal forgiveness and the power of the Spirit to pursue holiness.

The so-called salvation of the fleeing criminal actually corrupted the city of Ephesus by granting freedom to the wicked to continue in their perverse behavior. When the Ephesian Christians heard Jesus speak this promise to them in Revelation 2:7, they were able to appreciate, in a way that we can't, the concept of an eternal city pervaded and governed by the glory of God. For of *that* city, the New Jerusalem, not this-worldly Ephesus or any other city, it is said that "nothing unclean will ever enter it, nor anyone who does what is detestable or false, but only those who are written in the Lamb's book of life" (Rev. 21:27).

Oh, blessed cross, the only tree that truly brings life!

Part 2

The Church in Smyrna

To the angel of the church in Smyrna write: "The words of the first and the last, who died and came to life. I know your tribulation and your poverty (but you are rich) and the slander of those who say that they are Jews and are not, but are a synagogue of Satan. Do not fear what you are about to suffer. Behold, the devil is about to throw some of you into prison, that you may be tested, and for ten days you will have tribulation. Be faithful unto death, and I will give you the crown of life. He who has an ear, let him hear what the Spirit says to the churches. The one who conquers will not be hurt by the second death."

10

Seeing the "So That" in Suffering

Revelation 2:8–9

"To the angel of the church in Smyrna write: 'The words of the first and the last, who died and came to life.'"

A straight sail from the island of Patmos of approximately sixty miles brings one to the port of Ephesus at the mouth of the River Cayster. Traveling up coast some thirty-five miles almost due north of Ephesus is the city of Smyrna, population about one hundred thousand. It is the only one of the seven cities still in existence today, modern Izmir in western Turkey.

Smyrna was a proud and beautiful city and regarded itself as the "pride of Asia." An inscription on coins describes the city as "First of Asia in beauty and size" (although other cities were certainly more highly populated). The people of Smyrna were quite sensitive to the rivalry with Ephesus for recognition as the most splendid city of Asia Minor.

Of the seven churches, only Smyrna and Philadelphia receive no complaint from the Lord. There is only commendation, encouragement, and a promise of eternal life to the one who overcomes. Perhaps the reason there is no cause for complaint is that Smyrna was a suffering church. The letter is devoted almost exclusively to an account of their past and present trials, a warning of yet more persecution to come, and a strengthening word of encouragement from the One who knows all too well the pain of scorn and death.

It's of more than passing interest that the word *myrrh*, associated symbolically in the New Testament with weeping, burial, and resurrection, is related to the name of this city: Smyrna. But why did the church in Smyrna suffer? The answer is twofold.

First, as early as 195 B.C. a temple personified as a goddess and dedicated to Rome had been built in Smyrna. The city soon acquired a reputation for patriotic loyalty to the empire and its emperor. In A.D. 29 all Asian cities were competing for the coveted favor of erecting a temple in honor of Emperor Tiberius. Smyrna won. It was a city fervent with emperor worship.

The civil authorities didn't care so much that Christians worshiped Jesus, so long as they also worshiped the emperor. So when the believers in Smyrna refused to pay religious homage by sprinkling incense on the fire that burned before the emperor's bust, it no doubt fanned the flames of hostility against them. It was dangerous to be a faithful Christian in Smyrna!

Second, great antagonism existed within the Jewish community toward the church. This no doubt stemmed in part from their conviction that to worship a crucified carpenter from Nazareth was foolishness. Worse still, it was blasphemy (see especially 1 Cor. 1:18–25). There was also undoubtedly a measure of bitterness at the loss of so many from their ranks to the new faith.

The Jews were known to inform the authorities of Christian activities, the latter being perceived as treason. Jewish antagonism against Paul is well known in the book of Acts: at Antioch in 13:50; at Iconium in 14:2, 5; at Lystra in 14:19; at Thessalonica in 17:5; at Corinth they so bitterly opposed the gospel that Paul "shook out his garments and said to them, 'Your blood be on your own heads! I am innocent. From now on I will go to the Gentiles'" in 18:6.

Jewish opposition to the church at Smyrna is the focus of verse 9, where Jesus refers to those "who say that they are Jews and are not, but are a synagogue of Satan." Clearly, in one sense, these people *are* Jews, the physical descendants of Abraham, Isaac, and Jacob, who met regularly in the synagogue to worship. Yet, in another sense, i.e., inwardly and spiritually, they are *not* Jews, having rejected Jesus and now persecuting and slandering his people. Indeed, their gatherings at synagogue are energized by Satan himself. Yes, this is a harsh word, but it comes from Jesus and must be fully reckoned with.

But if they are false Jews, who, then, are the true Jews? If they are a synagogue of Satan, who, then, constitute the synagogue of God? John does not provide an explicit answer, but the implication seems clear. George Ladd explains:

> True Jews are the people of the Messiah. Paul says the same thing very clearly: "For he is not a real Jew who is one outwardly, nor is true circumcision something external and physical. He is a Jew who is one inwardly, and real circumcision is a matter of the heart, spiritual and not literal" (Rom. 2:28–29). That this "Judaism of the heart" is not to be limited to believing Jews but includes believing gentiles is clear from Paul's words to the Philippians: "For we are the true circumcision, who worship God in spirit, and glory in Christ Jesus" (Phil. 3:3). We must conclude, then, that John makes a real distinction between literal Israel—the Jews—and spiritual Israel—the church.[1]

What is of paramount importance, however, is that we see the relationship between suffering and sanctity. No one put it better or more to the point than Peter in his first epistle: "In this you rejoice, though now for a little while, if necessary, you have been grieved by various trials, so that the tested genuineness of your faith—more precious than gold that perishes though it is tested by fire—may be found to result in praise and glory and honor at the revelation of Jesus Christ" (1 Pet. 1:6–7).

This undoubtedly was true of the church at Smyrna. Trials are grievous, says Peter. Let no one pretend they are anything less than painful and distressing. But there is always a divine design in our suffering that, when seen and embraced, energizes the heart to persevere. Observe Peter's "so that" in verse 7a above. Praise be to God: there is always a "so that" in our suffering, always a higher spiritual end in view for the sake of which God orchestrates our troubles and trials.

Could this possibly be why the church in Smyrna escaped rebuke and was spared the threat of divine discipline addressed to the Ephesians? Had the "genuineness" of their "faith" been proven in (indeed, because of) the fire of affliction? Had the spurious and surface dimensions of their trust in God been burned away, leaving their faith as pure as gold, at least as pure as faith can be this side of heaven? Yes, I believe so.

Suffering isn't designed by God to destroy our faith but to intensify it. That will never happen, however, if we fail to look beyond the pain to the purpose of our loving heavenly Father. His design is to knock out from underneath us every false prop so that we might rely wholly on him. His aim is to create in us such desperation that we have nowhere else to look but to his promises and abiding presence.

There is, then, an alternative to cratering under the weight of distress. We need not yield either to *bitterness*, because things haven't gone our way, or to *doubt*, because we can't figure out God's ways, or to *anger*, because we feel abandoned. Rather, we can by his grace strive to see the "so that" in his mysterious and providential mercies. And even when we can't see it, we can trust him anyway!

11

Sustained by His Sovereignty

Revelation 2:8

"To the angel of the church in Smyrna write: 'The words of the first and the last, who died and came to life.'"

S uffering comes in many forms and in varying degrees, as the Christians in Smyrna would no doubt testify. But regardless of how it manifests itself, suffering tends to evoke one of two re-actions in the soul of the Christian: *dependency* or *disillusionment*.

One example of the former is found in the apostle Paul's reac-tion to a life-threatening incident that brought him to the brink of despair. Rather than yielding to disillusionment with God, he was driven to dependency upon him. The entire scenario, he later said, was "to make us rely not on ourselves but on God who raises the dead" (2 Cor. 1:9).

For many, however, disillusionment triumphs over dependency, often leading to a crippling bitterness that threatens both our en-joyment in life and our effectiveness in ministry. In using the word *ministry* I have in mind all believers here; not simply those we often call "clergy."

The reason for this, at least in part, is that suffering has a disorient-ing effect on the soul. What I mean is that pain, whether physical or emotional or both, contributes to a loss of perspective. We can see little else but the problem and its disruptive impact on every sphere of life. We feel lost and directionless, not knowing how to extricate ourselves from the mess we're in. There's no spiritual compass, so to speak, that points us to God and perhaps to some explanation for why we have to endure such unspeakable hurt.

This is why many who suffer experience deep disillusionment with God. "Doesn't he know what is happening? Doesn't he care? And if he does, why doesn't he do something about it? Maybe he's simply too busy or too weak." In any case, they feel lost at sea, adrift and carried hopelessly beyond the safety of the shore by wave after wave of disappointment and pain and shattered dreams and loss of friends and, well, whatever else it is that simply won't go away. To make sense of what is happening we need a point of reference, a "north star," as it were, to guide us back home and restore a measure of hope.

So how did Paul spiritually survive the "affliction" he "experienced in Asia" (2 Cor. 1:8)? Or better still, how did the Smyrnean Christians pull through, given all they were facing?

I'll return to the nature and extent of their suffering in the next meditation, but it surely entailed at least four dimensions. First, they were in the throes of "tribulation" and "poverty" (Rev. 2:9). These are so inextricably linked in the experience of the Christians in Smyrna that I list them as one. Again, more on the nature of this in the next lesson. Second, they were being slandered (2:9). Third, some of them were about to be imprisoned for their faith (2:10a). And fourth, some would even face martyrdom (2:10b).

My immediate concern is with how the Smyrneans avoided disillusionment, or better still, how Jesus himself proposed that they remain faithful and utterly dependent on God. We know they resisted the temptation to fall into despair or bitterness, but how? I suggest that at least part of the answer is found in the opening words of Jesus in his letter to them. In particular, it's found in how he is identified: "To the angel of the church in Smyrna write: 'The words of *the first and the last, who died and came to life*'" (2:8).

This description of Jesus is actually taken from the portrayal of him in Revelation 1. There John is granted a vision of the risen and glorified Lord, where Jesus himself declares: "Fear not, I am the first and the last, and the living one. I died, and behold I am alive forevermore, and I have the keys of Death and Hades" (vv. 17b–18).

So what possible difference could it make in their lives (or in ours) that Jesus is "the first and the last"? How does knowledge of that truth counteract the discombobulating effects of suffering? At first glance, knowing this about Jesus seems utterly irrelevant in the face of constant pain or financial loss or the breakdown of intimate relationships or, worst of all, the ominous prospect of physical death itself.

In fact, however, I suggest that nothing could more readily over-come disillusionment than knowledge of this truth. As I said earlier, suffering tends to bring disorientation to our hearts, a sense of being alone and lost and without a point of reference. Prolonged suffering breeds a feeling of chaos and loss of control. We ask: "Will I ever emerge from this dark tunnel? Is there an end in view? A purpose? Is there anything more ultimate than my own immediate discomfort that might enable me to persevere?"

Yes! In saying that he is the "first and the last" Jesus is affirming his comprehensive control over all of history, over every event that transpires within the parameters established by the terms *first* and *last*. As the one who is first, he is the source of all things. Nothing preceded him that might account for your suffering or suggest that it is outside the boundaries of his sovereign sway.

As the *last* he is the one toward whom all things are moving, the goal for which they exist, and the final explanation for all that is and occurs. Sufferers can look at their plight, feel their pain, calculate their losses, and still say: "But our Lord is the One who created it all, and he is the One for whom it is all being sustained and directed. My condition is not beyond the scope of his authority. He does have jurisdiction! Furthermore, if he is the *last*, if he is the one who stands as much on the back side of history as he did on the front end, then I know that what I'm enduring for his sake is not without purpose or fruit."

And what of the statement that he "died and came to life" (2:8)? A few have suggested that the people of Smyrna would have espe-cially appreciated this description of Jesus because of the city's own history. Smyrna was destroyed by the Lydians in 600 B.C., which was followed by three centuries of relative desolation until it was reestablished and rebuilt two miles south of the ancient site in 290 B.C. Well, maybe, but I think something else is involved that would prove even more significant to the suffering saints in that city.

Remember, they themselves were facing death. Martyrdom was a very real possibility (see Rev. 2:10). They needed to be reassured that physical death was nothing to fear, that it marked not the end but the beginning of true life, and that no matter how severe the suffering, they would *never* taste the "second death" (2:11) that awaits those who deny Jesus.

"Fear not," said Jesus to John in Revelation 1:17. Again, in 2:10 he declares, "Do not fear what you are about to suffer." This word of reassurance finds its basis in the fact that Jesus has conquered both sin and death. The believer need not fear either suffering or martyrdom, for Jesus has endured both and emerged victorious, and we are inseparably and eternally "in him."

Suffering is a given, an inescapable fact of life for the Christian. Its effects, on the other hand, are dependent on us. May God graciously energize our souls and enlighten our hearts that we, through the fog of anguish and disappointment, might see the light of his sovereignty, the one who is First and Last, who has died and come to life.

12

Having Nothing,
yet Possessing All

Revelation 2:9–10

"I know your tribulation and your poverty (but you are rich) and the slander of those who say that they are Jews and are not, but are a synagogue of Satan. Do not fear what you are about to suffer. Behold, the devil is about to throw some of you into prison, that you may be tested, and for ten days you will have tribulation. Be faithful unto death, and I will give you the crown of life."

As I sit writing this meditation, I need only turn my head slightly to the left and gaze out the window of my hotel room for a stunning view of the Washington Monument in our nation's capital. Two days earlier, on my way from the airport to the annual meeting of the Evangelical Theological Society, I was deeply moved by the site of the Lincoln Memorial, and later that night by the stunning profile of the Capitol building.

People react differently when visiting Washington DC. I have to confess that for a moment I found it all a bit disheartening, especially in view of the recent elections. But that was short-lived, for my mind was fixed on the Christians who lived, not in DC, but in ancient Smyrna. Those saints, whom Jesus commends here in Revelation 2:8–11, knew nothing of what I know. The freedoms and opportunities and legal protection under which I live and minister and so often sinfully take for granted were unknown to those believers.

What they faced in first-century Smyrna was as radically far-removed from what I now enjoy as one can possibly conceive.

I've already mentioned the suffering they experienced and its profoundly sanctifying results, but the time has come to look closely at precisely what they endured. Again, it's difficult for me to grasp what they awakened to each day. I've never known anything remotely similar, nor feared for my life, property, or family. That's due in large measure to the principles on which our country was founded, of which I was reminded by those buildings and structures in this remarkable city. But it doesn't prevent me from asking of my soul: "Sam, how would you have fared in Smyrna? Would Jesus have found anything commendable in your response to state-sponsored persecution? What if the power and authority of Washington DC were turned against you and your commitment to the gospel of Jesus Christ?"

Jesus singles out four dimensions of the suffering endured by the Smyrneans. Let's look briefly at each, not out of academic curiosity, but in order to ask ourselves: "Is my faith such that it would survive, indeed thrive, under such threats?"

First, reference is made in Revelation 2:9a to their "tribulation" and "poverty." But why were these believers poor in a city as prosperous as Smyrna? Perhaps they were from the lower ranks of society, economically speaking. It's possible they had exceeded their means in generous giving to others. But this would not explain why their poverty is part of their tribulation, and the association of the two words here indicates they are linked.

In some measure the poverty was due to their voluntary exclusion from the many trade guilds in Smyrna, seedbeds of vice, immorality, and unscrupulous business dealings. In addition, they probably struggled to find employment precisely because they were Christians. Most likely, however, as Hebrews 10:34 indicates, their homes and property had been looted and pillaged. As John Stott says, "Make no mistake: it does not always pay to be a Christian. Nor is honesty by any means always the best policy, if material gain is your ambition."[2]

Material gain was most assuredly *not* the ambition of the Smyrneans! I'm confident that, like those believers in Hebrews 10, they "joyfully accepted the plundering" of their "property," knowing that they "had a better possession and an abiding one" (v. 34). In the case of the Christians at Smyrna, they had riches their enemies couldn't understand, wealth that couldn't be stolen, possessions that weren't vulnerable to theft or rust or devaluation or falling stock prices. Indeed, despite their material poverty, Jesus declares that they are "rich" (Rev. 2:9).

Is this some sort of joke? Is Jesus toying with them? Hardly, for Paul said it best when he described himself and those who ministered at his side as "poor, yet making many rich; as having nothing, yet possessing everything" (2 Cor. 6:10). Did not James declare that God has "chosen those who are poor in the world to be *rich in faith and heirs of the kingdom*, which he has promised to those who love him" (James 2:5)?

Perhaps we should pause quietly and ask ourselves, "How do I measure *real* wealth? Is the treasure of knowing Jesus Christ of sufficient value that I regard myself as incomparably rich though I own little? Were I to lose everything but him, would I still consider myself blessed?"

Second, they were repeatedly slandered (v. 9a). Jesus doesn't specify the nature of this slander, literally, blasphemy, but I assume it included attacks on their character, mockery of their beliefs—"You put your trust in a crucified carpenter! Ha!"—and, most of all, hateful indignities heaped on their Lord.

Third, we read that some of them would be thrown into prison (v. 10). We must remember that imprisonment in Roman communities like Smyrna wasn't technically considered a punishment. Prisons were used for one of three reasons: (1) to compel and coerce obedience to the order of a magistrate; (2) to keep the accused confined pending the trial date; or (3) to detain the guilty until the time of execution. The words "until death" (v. 10b) indicate that the third is in view.

There are several options to interpreting the meaning of "ten days" of "tribulation." Some say it means literally ten days and leave it at that. Another view is that it simply refers to a short period of time, while others suggest that it points to extreme or complete tribulation. It's possible that Jesus had Daniel 1:12–15 in mind where the testing of Daniel and his three friends is said to be for ten days. Colin Hemer contends that "the 'ten days' should probably be seen as a limited, intermediate period of suffering, expected to terminate in judgment and death—but this for the Christian was victory and life, assured by the precedent of Christ's resurrection (cf. 1 Cor. 15:20)."[3]

Fourth, they were facing martyrdom itself. There's simply no escaping the fact that some of them would die. Yet Jesus does nothing to prevent it. He doesn't alleviate their poverty nor publicly vindicate his people in the face of those who hurled their indignant slander. And when Satan moves to incite their imprisonment and eventual execution, Jesus chooses not to intervene. There are certainly numerous instances in biblical days and in the history of the church when it was otherwise (see Heb. 11:32–34). But not always (see Heb. 11:35–38).

I've already addressed the issue, if only briefly, about why Christians suffer. But perhaps when we encounter such texts, our question should be of a different sort. Instead of asking, "Why do Christians suffer persecution?" we ought to inquire, "Why do Christians *not* suffer persecution?" John Stott put it pointedly: "The ugly truth is that we tend to avoid suffering by compromise. Our moral standards are often not noticeably higher than the standards of the world. Our lives do not challenge and rebuke unbelievers by their integrity or purity or love. The world sees in us nothing to hate."[4]

It's evening now, and the Washington Monument stands well lit against a darkened sky, a forceful reminder that, at least for now, the church is free to flourish in America. But that could change. I honestly don't worry much about it. I'm more concerned about whether in the face of tribulation and poverty I would consider myself rich.

King David declared, "You are my Lord; I have no good apart from you" (Ps. 16:2). Do you agree? Are other things good only because we have them from him and for his sake? I hope so. And if we lack such things, is he alone good enough that we regard ourselves as "possessing everything"? The Smyrneans did.

13

Faithfulness: The Fruit of Faith

Revelation 2:10

"Do not fear what you are about to suffer. Behold, the devil is about to throw some of you into prison, that you may be tested, and for ten days you will have tribulation. Be faithful unto death, and I will give you the crown of life."

To whom do you look for strength when life is on the verge of imploding and there seems to be no avenue of escape? In what do you place your trust? On what beliefs have you staked your future? How do you persevere?

Unless you've experienced an incredibly insulated life, these are questions that cannot be avoided. They were certainly questions racing through the minds of the believers in Smyrna. Their past had been painful and their immediate future didn't look promising. They had been slandered. Their reputation was shot, at least so far as the world was concerned. They'd suffered loss of home and property. What could possibly come next? Well, imprisonment and death to start with, or rather, to end with!

Jesus calls for our faithfulness in such circumstances no less than he called for theirs (v. 10). But it's not automatic. Endurance doesn't just happen. *Faithfulness is the fruit of faith.* In other words, there are truths we must embrace if we are to endure. Unbelief leads to bitterness and despair. Although Jesus chose not to intervene and deliver the Smyrneans from suffering, he by no means abandoned

69

them. Look with me again at his words of counsel, for in them is the power to persevere. There are three things to note.

First, I've already had occasion to mention how his knowledge of our situation is a source of strength: "*I know* your tribulation and your poverty" (v. 9a). Our knowledge of his knowledge of us is a powerful incentive to remain faithful when the world, flesh, and the devil conspire to yell, "Quit!" But there's more.

Second, observe closely that there are *divinely imposed limits* on how far Satan can go in his efforts to destroy us. For the Christians at Smyrna, not unlike the situation with Job, the enemy is given a long leash. But he can only go so far as God permits. Satan is unable to act outside the parameters established by the will of his Creator. In this case, he will instigate their incarceration, but only for ten days (v. 10).

"Wait a minute! How can you say that Satan is limited in what he can do if some of those he throws into prison end up getting killed?" That's a good question. Here's my answer. Just as there was a divinely imposed limitation on what Satan could perpetrate, there was a *divinely ordained purpose* for it: to test them (v. 10). In giving them over to the devil for imprisonment, and for some, death, God had not forsaken his people. This was not a sign of his disdain or rejection but a means by which to test and try and refine and purify their trust in Christ.

I find it incredibly instructive that what Satan intended for their destruction, God designed for their spiritual growth. Satan's intent was to undermine their faith, not to test it. Yet God orchestrated the entire scenario as a way of honing and stabilizing and solidifying the faith of the church in Smyrna.

We see much the same principle in Luke 22:31, where Jesus said, "Simon, Simon, behold, Satan demanded to have you, that he might sift you like wheat" (cf. 2 Cor. 12:7). Satan evidently obtained permission to tempt all of the disciples, for the "you" in verse 31 is plural. Whatever he had in mind for the others, his intent in sifting Peter in particular was obviously malicious, as he aimed to destroy the apostle by inciting him to deny Jesus. Perhaps he thought that the ensuing guilt and shame would paralyze Peter and disqualify him from ministry.

But God's goal was altogether different. His purposes with Peter were to instruct him, humble him, perhaps discipline him, and certainly to use him as an example to others of both human arrogance and the possibility of forgiveness and restoration. The point is simply that often we cannot easily say "Satan did it" or "God did it." In cases such as this, both are true, with the understanding that God's will is sovereign, supreme, and overriding, but their respective goals are clearly opposite. Sydney Page's comments concerning this incident are important:

> Luke 22:31–32 reveals that Satan can subject the loyalty of the followers of Jesus to severe tests that are designed to produce failure. So intense are the pressures to which Satan is able to subject believers that the faith of even the most courageous may be found wanting. Satan is, however, limited in what he can do by what God permits and by the intercession of Jesus on behalf of his own [cf. Rom. 8:34; Heb. 7:25; 1 John 2:1]. Furthermore, those who temporarily falter can be restored and, like Peter, can even resume positions of leadership. It is implied that Satan cannot gain ultimate victory over those for whom Jesus intercedes.[5]

The third encouraging thing for us to note is that the *death* Satan inflicts issues in *life* for the believer. In verse 10b Jesus encourages the Smyrneans to remain faithful unto physical death and he will give them "the crown of life." Jesus reminds them of this because he knows that the power to persevere comes from *a vibrant faith in the certainty of God's promised reward*. Those who do not love "their lives even unto death" (Rev. 12:11) are granted a "life" that infinitely transcends anything this earthly existence could ever afford. Jesus does not call for faithfulness unto death without reminding us that there awaits us in the future a quality and depth of true and unending life that far outweighs whatever sacrifice is made in the present.

This is precisely the point Paul made in 2 Corinthians 4:16–18. He refused to lose heart because he knew that "this light momentary affliction is preparing for us an eternal weight of glory beyond all comparison, as we look not to the things that are seen but to the things that are unseen. For the things that are seen are transient, but the things that are unseen are eternal."

Among the countless unseen things on which Paul fixed his faith was undoubtedly the certainty of the crown of life given to all who know Jesus. There is power to persevere in the promise of reward. We must intentionally lay hold of the future and impose it on the present. May God give us eyes to behold what we cannot see that we may hold fast to the faith and enter into life that is life indeed.

14

What I Deserve versus What I Get: Reflections on the "Second Death"

Revelation 2:11

"He who has an ear, let him hear what the Spirit says to the churches. The one who conquers will not be hurt by the second death."

The timing of this meditation is significant. I'm writing it on the day before Thanksgiving, 2006.

Like most of you, I'll soon be seated with my family around a table laden with more food than many people will see in a month. Thousands will die today of starvation. Tens of thousands will scrounge for a few kernels of corn or a handful of grain. No, I'm not trying to rob you of joy at this time of year. In fact, I'm trying to intensify it. You are not among those who go hungry, so rejoice. Be thankful!

No, I can't explain global hunger. Neither can you. But that is not my primary concern here, as important as that issue is in itself, and it *is* critically important. Rather, I was stirred to write this meditation upon reading the words of our Lord in Revelation 2:11. There he makes yet another stunning promise: "The one who conquers will not be hurt by the second death."

So, I want to talk about hell. That's right, hell. I know it is Thanksgiving, but what better time to think about hell and realize, "Oh, praise be to God that I will never go there!" I'm grateful for countless things, such as the meal I'll soon enjoy and the family with whom I'm blessed to share it. But let's pause for a moment and give thanks that those who know and love Jesus "will not be hurt by the second death."

The second death is mentioned three other times in Revelation, each of which reinforces the fact that this is Jesus' (and John's) way of referring to eternal punishment in the lake of fire. We read in Revelation 20:6, "Blessed and holy is the one who shares in the first resurrection! Over such the second death has no power, but they will be priests of God and of Christ, and they will reign with him for a thousand years." Later in the same chapter (v. 14), we are told that "Death and Hades were thrown into the lake of fire. This is the second death, the lake of fire." Finally, in Revelation 21:8 we read, "But as for the cowardly, the faithless, the detestable, as for murderers, the sexually immoral, sorcerers, idolaters, and all liars, their portion will be in the lake that burns with fire and sulfur, which is the second death."

Clearly, then, the second death is the lake of fire, the place of eternal torment for those who do not know and love our Lord Jesus Christ. The first death would be physical death, the death that Jesus said some in Smyrna would suffer because of their faith in him. The point of his promise, then, is this: no matter how much you may endure physically in the present, you will never suffer spiritually in the future. Therefore, be faithful if you should be called on to die *now*, for you will never die *then*!

The contrasts couldn't be more vivid. Those who know and love Jesus and remain faithful to him will be granted the "crown of life" (v. 10). They will never, by no means ever—such is the literal force of the double negative in Greek—taste the "second death" (v. 11).

Now, hear me well. There is nothing of which I am more deserving than the second death. There is nothing more fitting, more just, more righteous than that I should suffer forever in the lake of fire. And the only reason why I won't is that Jesus has endured in himself the judgment it entails. Jesus has exhausted in his own person the wrath of God that I otherwise would have faced in the lake of fire.

As I reflect on that reality I can't help but feel complete dismay at those who reject penal substitutionary atonement, or flippantly and blasphemously dismiss it as "cosmic child abuse." What hope have we for deliverance from the second death if not the suffering of its pains, in our stead, by the Son of God? If I receive the crown of life, which I don't deserve, in place of the lake of fire, which I do deserve, it can only be for one reason: Jesus Christ, by a marvelous and ineffable exchange, has died that I might live, has suffered that I might be set free, has for me faced and felt the wrath of God and absorbed it in himself.

I suppose some might still seek to undermine the force of Revelation 2:11 by simply denying that the second death is equivalent to the lake of fire. Many today are doing precisely that, as they cleverly and subversively deny that Jesus ever believed in or taught, much less endured in his own person, the reality of hell's torments. What "gospel," then, can they preach? In what does the good news consist if not that Jesus has died, the just for the unjust, having "redeemed us from the curse of the law by becoming a curse for us" (Gal. 3:13)?

As for the Christians in Smyrna, no sweeter words were ever spoken than these. Tribulation was tolerable, knowing that the second death died in the death of Jesus. Slander and imprisonment, yes, even martyrdom, were but "light momentary affliction" when compared with the "eternal weight of glory" (2 Cor. 4:17) that is ours because Jesus died and rose again on our behalf.

Yes, thinking about hell and the second death has immense practical benefits. In his famous *Resolutions*, Jonathan Edwards put it succinctly: "Resolved, when I feel pain, to think of the pains of martyrdom, and of hell" (no. 10).

It is remarkable how tolerable otherwise intolerable things become when we see them in the light of the second death. *Think often, then, of the pains of hell. Think often, I say, of the lake of fire.* It puts mere earthly pain in perspective. It puts tribulation and poverty and slander and imprisonment and even death itself in their proper place. The collective discomfort of all such temporal experience is nothing in comparison with the eternal torment of the second death in the lake of fire.

The one who conquers, said Jesus, "will not be hurt by the second death." Not even when Satan viciously accuses me of sins we all know I've committed? No, never, by no means ever will I be hurt by the second death. Not even when others remind me of how sinful I still am, falling short of the very standards I loudly preach and proclaim? No, never, by no means ever will I be hurt by the second death. Not even when my own soul screams in contempt at the depravity of my heart? No, never, by no means ever will I be hurt by the second death.

And that for one reason only: Jesus, in unfathomable mercy and grace, has suffered that hurt in my place.

So, be faithful, Christian man or woman. Rejoice, oh child of God. And give thanks that you will never, by no means ever, suffer harm from the second death!

The Church in Pergamum

And to the angel of the church in Pergamum write: "The words of him who has the sharp two-edged sword. I know where you dwell, where Satan's throne is. Yet you hold fast my name, and you did not deny my faith even in the days of Antipas my faithful witness, who was killed among you, where Satan dwells. But I have a few things against you: you have some there who hold the teaching of Balaam, who taught Balak to put a stumbling block before the sons of Israel, so that they might eat food sacrificed to idols and practice sexual immorality. So also you have some who hold the teaching of the Nicolaitans. Therefore repent. If not, I will come to you soon and war against them with the sword of my mouth. He who has an ear, let him hear what the Spirit says to the churches. To the one who conquers I will give some of the hidden manna, and I will give him a white stone, with a new name written on the stone that no one knows except the one who receives it."

15

Satan's City

Revelation 2:12–13

"And to the angel of the church in Pergamum write: 'The words of him who has the sharp two-edged sword. I know where you dwell, where Satan's throne is.'"

By God's providential design, my wife and I live in Kansas City, Missouri, known as "The City of Fountains." Before this, we lived in Chicago, "The Windy City." Well, to be more accurate, we lived in Winfield, a suburb of Chicago. Paris, France, is called "The City of Lights," and New York is often described as "The City That Never Sleeps." We have friends who live in Las Vegas, infamously but justifiably referred to as "Sin City," and the list could go on.

So what's the point? Simply this: from what Jesus says in his letter to the church in Pergamum, the Christians there may well be described as living in "Satan's City." "I know where you dwell," said Jesus, "where Satan's throne is" (Rev. 2:13a). Later in the same verse he refers to Pergamum as the place "where Satan dwells" (Rev. 2:13b).

Let's get to know the city of Pergamum, after which we'll return to our Lord's reassuring words: "I know where you dwell."

Pergamum was one of the largest cities in the ancient world, with a population of about 190,000. It was situated about sixty-five miles due north of Smyrna and exceeded its southern neighbor both in love for and loyalty to the emperor. Pergamum was the capital city of the Roman province of Asia and retained this honor well into the second century. But it wasn't primarily for either political or economic achievements that Pergamum was famous, but for *religion*. Pergamum was the center of worship for at least four of the most important pagan cults of the day.

Upon entering the city one couldn't help but notice the gigantic altar of Zeus erected on a huge platform some eight hundred feet above the city, looking down on its inhabitants like a great vulture hovering over its prey. Many have sought to identify "Satan's seat" or "throne" (v. 13) with this altar. Amazingly, a reconstructed form of this altar is on display in the Pergamum Museum in Berlin, which I had the privilege [?] of visiting in 1994.

Pergamum was also the center for the worship of Athene and Dionysus. However, the most distinctive and celebrated cult of all was dedicated to the worship of Asclepios, or Aesculapius. Often referred to as "Savior" (*soter*) in Greek mythology, Asclepios was the son of Apollo and was thought to have been the very first physician. The symbol of Asclepios was the serpent, which has led some to identify the "throne of Satan" with the shrine erected to his worship. You might also recall that the symbol adopted by the U.S. Department of Health, Education, and Welfare, renamed The Department of Health and Human Services in 1979, is the staff of Asclepios with a serpent coiled around it.

But above and beyond the worship directed at these pagan deities was the fact that Pergamum was the acknowledged center in Asia Minor for the imperial cult of Caesar. In 29 B.C. this city received permission to build and dedicate a temple to Augustus, three years before Smyrna was granted a similar privilege. Perhaps more than any of the other six cities, the people of Pergamum were devoted to the worship of Caesar.

Were it not for the fact that greater is he who is in us than he who is in the world (1 John 4:4b), it would be frightening to hear that Pergamum is "where Satan dwells" (Rev. 2:13b). Although this may simply be synonymous with "Satan's throne" (v. 13a), it's possible that this is another way of saying that evil was present in Pergamum in a particularly powerful and concentrated way. Could it be that Satan had in some sense made Pergamum the focus of his earthly base of operation?

Needless to say, Jesus knew this. On second thought, it *does* need to be said. To those believers immersed in an explicitly Satanic atmosphere of idolatry and wickedness, Jesus says: "I know where you dwell!" To a people struggling by grace to remain faithful when those around them revel in faithlessness, Jesus says: "I know where you dwell!" To a church that must, at times, have felt abandoned and alone and given over to the enemy, Jesus says: "I know where you dwell!"

We have already seen that our Lord knows the churches, for he walks among them (Rev. 2:1). In this letter, however, "He makes it clear that His intimate knowledge extends not only to the works His people do (as in Ephesus) and to the tribulation they endure (as in Smyrna) but to *the environment in which they live.* 'I know where you dwell,' He says. He is not ignorant of the fact that the Christian Church is set in the non-Christian world, and that it feels on all sides the continuous pressure of heathen influence."[1]

Jesus was fully aware that Pergamum, of all the cities in Asia Minor, would be most severely threatened by pagan influence. Thus the place "where Satan's throne is" (v. 13) most likely refers to the primary role of Pergamum as the center of the imperial cult and as such the center of Satan's kingdom in the east if not beyond as well.

The fact that "throne" has the definite article "the" indicates that Jesus is referring to a specific throne, whether literal or figurative, which he expects the people of Pergamum to recognize. In Revelation 13:2 it says that Satan gave the "beast . . . his throne and great authority" (cf. 16:10). If nothing else, this suggests that Satan works through the ungodly, earthly political power in Pergamum to persecute and oppress God's people.

The most prominent visible feature of Pergamum was the acropolis, a heavily fortified fortress that rose nearly thirteen hundred feet above the plain. Some have argued that it actually looks like a great throne when seen by a traveler approaching from Smyrna. However, as Colin Hemer points out, this is "only a picturesque association which might appeal to a modern visitor without necessarily relating to an ancient reality."[2] In any case, the Christians at Pergamum went to bed each night and awakened each morning to a relentless and pervasive idolatry in a city that had willfully "exchanged the glory of the immortal God for images resembling mortal man and birds and animals and reptiles" (Rom. 1:23).

Here's what I want you to understand: Jesus also knows where *you* dwell. Don't dismiss it as a theological truism. I can assure you, the oppressed believers in Pergamum didn't. They laid hold of that glorious revelation and drew from it the refreshing waters of reassurance and hope and confidence. They would often, no doubt, remind themselves that no matter how hard it was to be a Christian there, no matter how intense the temptation to abandon Christ and serve another god, Jesus knew where they lived, he knew what they faced on a daily basis, and he knew every intimate detail of a life pursued in a city that hated God.

Jesus knows where you dwell. Meditate on it. Rejoice in it! Whether you live in an isolated Midwestern town of five thousand or feel lost in a metropolis of five million, Jesus knows where you live. Whether you attend, or perhaps serve as pastor of, a congregation of fifty or a mega-church of five thousand, Jesus knows where you dwell. He knows the temptations you face, the pressures you feel, the fear that perhaps you've been misplaced or marginalized or lost in the shuffle of life and the countless concerns that our Lord must deal with on a daily basis. Fear not! Jesus knows where you dwell.

You haven't been abandoned, far less ignored. Your life and ministry are as important to Jesus as that of any Christian in any church in any city in any country. You may feel as if your community is a modern Pergamum, devoted to idolatry and immorality and the public ridicule of our glorious Savior. But of this you can rest assured: Jesus has *sovereignly* and *strategically* placed you there as his witness, to hold forth his name and to display his glory. That is why, contrary to the title of this meditation, every city is Christ's City. Jesus knows where you dwell.

16

Wonderful Words of Life— and Death

Revelation 2:12

"And to the angel of the church in Pergamum write: 'The words of him who has the sharp two-edged sword.'"

The letter to the church at Pergamum consists of "the words of him who has the sharp two-edged sword" (Rev. 2:12); more literally, "*these things says* the one who has the sharp two-edged sword."

When we hear or read of someone who has a sharp two-edged sword we typically envision it in his *hand*, to be wielded either in defense against an oncoming attack or used offensively to slay his enemies. But in the case of Jesus, the sword proceeds from his *mouth*. Although the mouth of our Lord isn't explicitly mentioned in Revelation 2:12, the description of him here is taken from the vision given to John in Revelation 1:16 where we read, "In his right hand he held seven stars, from his mouth came a sharp two-edged sword, and his face was like the sun shining in full strength" (1:16).

Similar language is used again in Revelation 19:15 and 19:21. There we read of Jesus' coming at the end of history to bring judgment on his enemies: "From his mouth comes a sharp sword with which to strike down the nations, and he will rule them with a rod of iron. He will tread the winepress of the fury of the wrath of God the Almighty" (19:15). And again, "the rest were slain by the sword that came from the mouth of him who was sitting on the horse, and all the birds were gorged with their flesh" (19:21; cf. Isa. 11:4).

This is clearly figurative language, for not even the crassest literalist would argue that there is a literal sword proceeding out of the literal mouth of Jesus. But to say it is figurative is not in any way to diminish the very real point that the words of Jesus are an infinitely powerful force not only in the defense and building up of his people but also in the judgment and destruction of his enemies.

The reference to a sword in this passage (Rev. 2:12) carried special significance for the Christians in Pergamum, given the fact that the sword was the symbol of the Roman proconsul's total sovereignty "over every area of life, especially to execute enemies of the state (called *ius gladii*). . . . This tells the church that it is the exalted Christ, not Roman officials, who is the true judge. The ultimate power belongs to God, and nothing the pagans can do will change that."[3]

But the words of Jesus are also designed to strengthen and encourage and edify his people. This is clear from the sevenfold refrain, "He who has an ear, let him hear what the Spirit says to the churches" (Rev. 2:7, 11, 17, 29; 3:6, 13, 22). The voice of Jesus and of the Spirit to the seven churches is one, a singular witness designed to commend, rebuke, instruct, and induce repentance.

And of course we mustn't forget Hebrews 4:12, where the word of God is described as "living and active, sharper than any *two-edged sword*, piercing to the division of soul and of spirit, of joints and of marrow, and discerning the thoughts and intentions of the heart" (Heb. 4:12).

The Christians in Pergamum (and we) should take courage from this truth. The Lord Jesus who knows where they dwell, who knows the struggles they face and the seductive appeal of a pagan environment, has words of life and hope for them, words that when heard and heeded bring wisdom and endurance and the power to resist the enemy who dwelt so powerfully in their midst.

But the sword that proceeds from his mouth is not only sharp; it is "two-edged" (v. 13). In other words, it cuts both ways. It is not only an instrument of life, but of judgment and death as well.

On the one hand, this sword has the power to perform the most delicate of spiritual surgery, to excise the cancer of sin and restore hope to the wounded soul. Its razor's edge cuts away the disease of error in those who long for truth. But to those who deny its authority, or acknowledge its presence but mock its power and purity, it is the means by which they will be called to account. The other side of the two-edged sword cuts away all excuses, identifies all sin, exposes the secrets of the soul, pronounces a just verdict, and issues and enforces an eternal sentence.

The apostle Paul spoke of this dual function of the word of Christ as made known in the gospel itself. When we faithfully preach and embody the truth of the cross, one of two things will happen: "For we are the aroma of Christ to God among those who are being saved and among those who are perishing, *to one a fragrance from death to death, to the other a fragrance from life to life*" (2 Cor. 2:15–16).

Those who hear this message are divided into two, and only two, groups: those who are being saved and those who are perishing (see 1 Cor. 1:18). The message of Christ that Paul proclaims is itself responsible for dividing the hearers in this way. Neutrality is not an option. To the one, Paul's message is a pleasing perfume. Like spiritual oxygen, it infuses life into their hearts. To the other, it is a vile stench in their spiritual nostrils, a suffocating and toxic fume that leads only to death.

Charles Spurgeon reminds us:

> The gospel is preached in the ears of all; it only comes with power to some. The power that is in the gospel does not lie in the eloquence of the preacher; otherwise men would be converters of souls. Nor does it lie in the preacher's learning; otherwise it would consist in the wisdom of men. We might preach till our tongues rotted, till we should exhaust our lungs and die, but never a soul would be converted unless there were mysterious power going with it—the Holy Ghost changing the will of man. O Sirs! We might as well preach to stone walls as to preach to humanity unless the Holy Ghost be with the Word, to give it power to convert the soul.[4]

The church in Pergamum was in desperate need of the power of Christ's words. On the one hand, they were sorely tempted to abandon the faith. Death had already come to one of their number (see Rev. 2:13) and others no doubt faced a similar fate. Christ's words were designed to strengthen their resolve and satisfy their souls lest they be drawn to another lover.

For the faint, his words are perfect, reviving the soul (Ps. 19:7a). For the confused, they are sure, bringing wisdom and enlightenment (Ps. 19:7b; 8b). For the saddened, his words are right, rejoicing the heart (Ps. 19:8a). His words are to be desired more than gold, even much fine gold (Ps. 19:10a). They are sweeter than honey and the drippings of the honeycomb (Ps. 19:10b). By his words we are warned and in keeping them there is great reward (Ps. 19:11). Only in hearing, cherishing, and faithfully keeping Christ's utterances will our own words, together with the meditation of our hearts, be acceptable in the sight of our great God, our rock and our redeemer (Ps. 19:14).

17

A Paradox in Pergamum

Revelation 2:13

"I know where you dwell, where Satan's throne is. Yet you hold fast my name, and you did not deny my faith even in the days of Antipas my faithful witness, who was killed among you, where Satan dwells."

There was in the church at Pergamum a strange and unacceptable paradox, an inconsistency that Jesus simply will not tolerate, then or now.

Let's not forget where they lived. Whereas it is true that "the whole world lies in the power of the evil one" (1 John 5:19b), Pergamum was especially vulnerable to Satan's influence. In some sense, as previously noted, this was *his* city. Pergamum was the center of his authority, the place of his throne, the focal point of his activity and interests. There must have been an almost tangible sense of his presence, a heaviness in the air, an oppressive spiritual atmosphere that was unmistakable and inescapable.

There have been times and places when I was keenly aware of an extraordinary spiritual darkness, all physical evidence to the contrary. In other words, a city, for example, can be outwardly prosperous, socially vibrant, and culturally sophisticated and all the while an underlying demonic energy animates and defiles its life and ethos. We shouldn't be surprised that our enemy might choose to concentrate his efforts in particular geographical areas or at unique and critical moments in history. It's all part of his strategy to undermine Christian faith and promote the kingdom of darkness.

The Christians in Pergamum undoubtedly faced this phenomenon every day. The corrupt political life of their community, the pagan temples that dotted the landscape, the resistance they encountered every time they shared their faith with an unsaved neighbor, all reminded them of Satan's intensified efforts to exert his authority in their midst.

That the church had refused to yield to such pressures or allowed their witness to fall silent is remarkable indeed. Our Lord's commendation of them for this comes in two forms.

He first applauds them for continuing to hold fast his name, i.e., his identity as God incarnate and his redemptive work at Calvary, in spite of the presence of Satan's throne (Rev. 2:13a; cf. the use of this verb, "hold fast," in Heb. 4:14; 10:23). On this point there can be no compromise, not even in the name of love. His use of the present tense of the verb indicates that even then, at the time they received this letter, they continue to maintain their testimony and were refusing to silence their voice for the sake of personal safety.

How often do we today, in public, speak in a hushed whisper when the name of Jesus is mentioned? What accounts for this? Could it be shame or embarrassment, or the prospect of losing face? I think it more likely that silence is driven by our *fear* of what might happen should those around us detect that we are Christians. It's remarkable, actually, given the fact that we face no persecution to speak of, no official resistance from our government. Yet, the Christians at Pergamum knew that a vocal public witness to the name of Jesus guaranteed precisely that, and worse.

I say *worse* because of what we read in the second half of verse 13. Not only were they presently holding forth a public testimony of the name of Jesus, but in the past also they had refused to deny their faith in spite of the martyrdom of an outspoken Christian named Antipas. Jesus commends them because they "did not deny my faith even in the days of Antipas my faithful witness, who was killed among you, where Satan dwells" (Rev. 2:13b).

Several things should be noted here. In the first place, Antipas is called a "faithful witness" (v. 13b), pointing no doubt to what led to his death. The Greek term *martus*, here translated "witness," refers to someone who bears verbal testimony to the person and work of Jesus. Initially the term described someone who provided information in a court of law. In time it was applied to that person whose Christian faith in court led to his or her execution. And thus eventually the word *witness* gave way wholly to the concept of martyrdom, death brought upon someone who offered persistent testimony for the sake of the kingdom, whether in or out of court.

A second important point to note is that the believers in Pergamum held fast to their faith "even in the days of Antipas." The ESV translates it this way, rightly so in my opinion, to highlight the fact that there were life-threatening circumstances that might have made their silence a matter of prudence. Who could have blamed them, from a worldly perspective, that is, had they chosen to keep their mouths shut, or perhaps even deny Jesus altogether? But no, they didn't let the prospect of their own martyrdom close their mouths or diminish their commitment or mollify their zeal.

Thirdly, what they are specifically said not to have denied is "the faith of me." This odd phrase should probably be rendered "faith *in* me," pointing to their unyielding and sturdy confidence in Jesus and the truth of his gospel.

However, as noted earlier, there was something askew in Pergamum. Notwithstanding their remarkable devotion to the Lord, they had become overly tolerant of others whose immorality threatened to undermine the purity of the church. If the Ephesian church was guilty of elevating truth above love, the church at Pergamum had elevated love above truth. Their commitment to peace and tolerance had apparently degenerated into a weak sentimentality that now posed both a serious ethical and theological threat.

Following our Lord's commendation he quickly adds a word of complaint. Whereas they had maintained their own theological convictions, they were, at the same time, tolerating in their fellowship certain false prophets who advocated licentious behavior, ostensibly in the name of Christian freedom (see vv. 14–15). This simply will not do.

Although they had not themselves denied the faith, they had become inexplicably lax toward falsehood in the assembly and had endured the presence and teaching of ethical error. For this,

Jesus severely rebukes them (which we'll take up in subsequent meditations).

This is a truly remarkable, indeed puzzling, situation. They were devoted to the truth of who Christ is and the essentials of the gospel message. They were even willing to die for it! But they fudged when it came to dealing with those in the church who compromised the ethical implications of that very gospel. It's almost as if they said, "I personally will never back down, even if it means my death. On the other hand, perhaps we need to be less rigid and a bit more tolerant when it comes to those who draw different conclusions about the practical implications of the saving grace of our Lord."

"No!" said Jesus. This is horribly inconsistent and must be immediately and firmly addressed (see v. 16). There's nothing to indicate why they had adopted this posture. It certainly wasn't out of fear. Perhaps they reckoned that such ethical and theological deviations were of little consequence or that they could more easily win over the dissidents by declining to rock the ecclesiological boat. Whatever the case, they were misguided in granting them such a wide berth and must act swiftly to put things right.

The bottom line is this: *sometimes peace and love come at too high a price.* In the next meditation we'll look more closely at the price the Christians at Pergamum had mistakenly paid.

18

How High the Price of Purity?

Revelation 2:14–16

"But I have a few things against you: you have some there who
hold the teaching of Balaam, who taught Balak to put a stumbling block before the sons of Israel, so that they might eat food
sacrificed to idols and practice sexual immorality. So also you
have some who hold the teaching of the Nicolaitans. Therefore
repent. If not, I will come to you soon and war against them with
the sword of my mouth."

Although grace is surely amazing, it is also subject to distor-
tion, especially by those who use it to excuse loose and
licentious behavior (see Gal. 5:13; Jude 4). The justification
comes in a variety of forms. For example: "If all my sins have been
forgiven, they are now of little consequence." Or again: "If I can't
be saved by works, I need not be concerned with their absence in
my life." Still others say: "If Jesus has set me free, I'm obligated to
no law or leader." Perhaps the most egregious expression of such
justification was stated rhetorically by Paul himself in Romans 6:1:
"What shall we say then? Are we to continue in sin that grace may
abound?" God forbid!

The church at Pergamum was infested with people who thought
in precisely such terms. They were called Nicolaitans. In an earlier
meditation I suggested that they were evidently licentious and antinomian and advocated an unhealthy compromise with pagan society

and the idolatrous culture of Ephesus. Now we see that they were present in Pergamum as well.

But there was a difference in the response to the Nicolaitans in these two congregations. According to Revelation 2:6, the Ephesians hated the work of the Nicolaitans and refused to tolerate their pernicious behavior. The Pergamemes, on the other hand, had welcomed them into the fellowship of the church and given them freedom to propagate their destructive ways.

There's no indication these false teachers had openly denied the "name" to which the others at Pergamum held fast. In other words, I doubt if the error of the Nicolaitans was a denial of the incarnation of Christ, his propitiatory work on the cross, or his bodily resurrection. Rather, as noted above, they were guilty of turning the grace of God into licentiousness. But let's look more closely at the error of their ways.

How serious was their presence in the church at Pergamum? Serious enough to provoke Jesus to say: "I have a few things against you" (Rev. 2:14a). That ought to alert us to the depths of this problem. He describes them as holding to "the teaching of Balaam, who taught Balak to put a stumbling block before the sons of Israel, so that they might eat food sacrificed to idols and practice sexual immorality. So also you have some who hold the teaching of the Nicolaitans" (Rev. 2:14–15).

We read of Balaam in Numbers 22–24. Balak, king of Moab, had solicited Balaam to curse the children of Israel who were preparing to cross over into the Promised Land. But God intervened. Every time Balaam spoke, words of blessing came forth. Moved by greed for the reward Balak offered him, Balaam advised Balak that Moabite women should seduce the men of Israel by inviting them to partake in their idolatrous feasts, which invariably led to sexual immorality. Balaam knew that this would provoke the judgment of God against his people, which is precisely what happened.

What Balaam was to the children of Israel in the Old Testament, the Nicolaitans were to the church of Jesus Christ in the New. Balaam is a prototype of those who promote compromise with the world in idolatry and immorality (see also Jude 11 and 2 Pet. 2:15). The Nicolaitans had dared to insinuate that freedom in Christ granted them a blank check to sin. The fault of the Pergamemes was not so much that they had followed this pernicious teaching but that they had allowed it be vocalized in the congregation. This matter of indifference to the licentiousness of the Nicolaitans was of grave concern to the risen Lord.

What is the precise nature of their sin? They put a stumbling block in the way of God's people "so that they might eat food sacrificed to idols and practice sexual immorality" (v. 14). The former probably refers to eating food sacrificed to idols *in the context of idolatrous worship*. Perhaps, then, the Nicolaitans were advocating, in the name of Christian freedom, participation in the worship service both of the local church and the local pagan temple. A similar problem existed at Corinth (see 1 Cor. 10:14–22). They evidently weren't in the least bothered by such compromise.

And what of the reference to the practice of sexual immorality? Often in the Old Testament spiritual idolatry was described metaphorically in terms of prostitution and sexual immorality (see Jer. 3:2; 13:27; Ezek. 16:15–58; 23:1–49; 43:7; Hos. 5:4; 6:10). In Revelation, to fornicate (*porneuo*) and its cognates usually are metaphorical for spiritual apostasy and idol worship (14:8; 17:1, 2, 4, 5, 15, 16; 18:3, 9; 19:2). When these words are used literally, they are part of vice lists (9:21; 21:8; 22:15).

However, we can't dismiss the possibility that the Nicolaitans were teaching that forgiveness of sin and their newfound freedom in Christ have now released them from what they regarded as "slavish obedience" to rules and regulations concerning sexual conduct. How tragic that today we still hear such arguments in the defense of both heterosexual and homosexual immorality.

But why not just live and let live? Is it really necessary that the faithful in Pergamum confront these libertines? Why rock the boat? Doesn't Christian love call for tolerance and minding our own business?

I'll let the words of Jesus answer those questions: "Therefore repent. If not, I will come to you soon and war against them with the sword of my mouth" (Rev. 2:16).

Two things deserve comment. First, the repentance Jesus calls for entails immediate acknowledgment of the error in their thinking and the lack of courage in their stance regarding the antinomians. "Recognize and confess," says Jesus, "that you are doing no one a favor by overlooking and allowing such sin in your midst! Confronting the Nicolaitans may be uncomfortable for you, even painful, but not nearly as painful as the judgment they will suffer if they remain in their sin." This call to repentance may also include the ultimate expulsion from the church of the Nicolaitans should they choose not to respond favorably.

Second, notice that Jesus says "I will come to *you*" soon, but will "war against *them*." The faithful at Pergamum aren't off the hook. If they don't repent Jesus will bring discipline against them, in precisely what form we aren't told. But the Nicolaitans will be the focus of judgment. It is against them that Jesus will make war. Such language suggests that their lack of repentance would be evidence of a lack of saving faith. Their persistent licentiousness and morally compromising behavior undermines their claim to know Jesus in a saving way.

The Christians in Pergamum had sacrificed the ethical purity of their congregation on the altar of "love" and for the sake of some nebulous peace they feared to lose. Purity often comes at an extremely high price. But we must be prepared to pay it. Confrontation is never pleasant, but it often reaps a bountiful harvest. By all means, pursue love, but not at the expense of truth or in such a way that overt sin is left to fester and spread in the body of Christ.

19

Jesus *Is* the Feast

Revelation 2:17

"He who has an ear, let him hear what the Spirit says to the churches. To the one who conquers I will give some of the hidden manna, and I will give him a white stone, with a new name written on the stone that no one knows except the one who receives it."

I suggested in the previous meditation that purity often comes with a hefty price tag. It may cost us good feelings and appear to be less than loving when we insist on repentance and moral rectitude. There's no way around the fact that peace and harmony may suffer when we are committed to living out the ethical implications of the gospel of grace. But, as I said, it's a price we must be willing to pay.

To some, that may sound depressing. It shouldn't. Yes, it's true that in the immediate present there will be some attendant pain when hard decisions are made and morally compromising behavior is confronted. But look at what Jesus promises in the long run for those who are obedient, i.e., for those who conquer (Rev. 2:17) by repenting from such "sloppy agape" and refuse to participate with or permit the teaching of the Nicolaitans. They will receive "some of the hidden manna" (Rev. 2:17), as well as "a white stone, with a new name written on the stone that no one knows except the one who receives it" (Rev. 2:17).

Perhaps that doesn't strike you as much of an incentive, but I suspect it will once we dig more deeply into the meaning of this promise.

Our Lord's reference to the manna may well be due to his earlier mention of Balaam, in whose time Israel was being fed with manna from heaven, and according to Jewish tradition, precious stones fell along with the manna.

Hebrew tradition records that a pot of manna was preserved in the ark of the covenant (Ex. 16:32–34; Heb. 9:4). According to 2 Maccabees 2:4–7, when the temple was destroyed in 586 B.C., either Jeremiah or an angel supposedly rescued the ark, together with the manna, both of which would be preserved underground on Mount Sinai until the messianic age, when the manna would again become the food for God's people. When the Messiah would come, Jeremiah would reappear and deposit both ark and manna in the new temple in Jerusalem.

But the manna, most assuredly, is Jesus himself. Let's look again in John 6 at his stunning claim.

> "Our fathers ate the manna in the wilderness; as it is written, 'He gave them bread from heaven to eat.'" Jesus then said to them, "Truly, truly, I say to you, it was not Moses who gave you the bread from heaven, but my Father gives you the true bread from heaven. For the bread of God is he who comes down from heaven and gives life to the world." They said to him, "Sir, give us this bread always." Jesus said to them, "I am the bread of life; whoever comes to me shall not hunger, and whoever believes in me shall never thirst. . . . I am the bread of life. Your fathers ate the manna in the wilderness, and they died. This is the bread that comes down from heaven, so that one may eat of it and not die. I am the living bread that came down from heaven. If anyone eats of this bread, he will live forever. And the bread that I will give for the life of the world is my flesh." (John 6:31–35, 48–51)

The promise to those who conquer in Revelation 2:17, therefore, is the assurance that they will feast forever on the person of Christ. That's a wonderful thought, a moving metaphor, but what does it mean?

It means that Jesus, and only Jesus, will be the sustenance of our body and soul for all eternity. On him alone shall we spiritually feed and draw strength. He is the source of our ongoing and eternal life. We are forever dependent on the infusion of his grace and mercy, upheld in existence by the exertion of his marvelous power.

It means we will experience, in relation with him, depths of intimacy utterly inconceivable in our present state of being. Our fallen minds cannot conceive the dimensions of spiritual ecstasy that await us in the ages to come. Our deceitful hearts cannot fathom the spiritual joy we'll feel forever as the magnitude of his affection for us is made known afresh each moment of each passing day.

It means that when it comes to our knowledge of his personality and the glory and wisdom of his ways, words such as *consummation* and *termination* and *completion* will be utterly out of place. The revelation of his character will be eternally incessant. The display of heretofore unknown facets of his beauty will suffer no lack.

It means that we will never grow weary of seeing his splendor or become bored with the disclosure of his grace. Jesus, as the manna of eternal life, will be an infinite supply of refreshment and joy and affirmation and delight.

It means that just as eating now brings a physical satisfaction, as hunger pains are silenced and cravings are met, so the "bread of life" will satisfy our souls and enrich our resurrected bodies and fascinate our glorified minds beyond our wildest and most outrageous dreams.

It means that Jesus will be for us an endless, self-replenishing spring of refreshing water, an inexhaustible, infinitely abundant source of excitement and intrigue, an eternal, ever-increasing database of knowledge and insight and discovery that will never diminish in its capacity to enthrall and captivate.

It means that because of Jesus, and Jesus alone, we will experience the odd but glorious sensation of never being deficient but always desiring increase, of ever being filled but constantly hungry for more.

In our current condition, fallen and frail as we are, we lack the faculties to grasp such truths. They seem so experientially remote, so far beyond our capacity to see or touch or feel or even dream, that we easily dismiss them as flights of rhetorical fancy. Neither can our minds conceive nor can our hearts envision such depths of delight and beauty. What does incessantly increasing joy feel like?

How does one describe ever-expanding excitement? Can one truly experience eternally accelerating affections of love and adoration?

Once again, I defer to Jonathan Edwards. When asked these questions, his answer was that "without doubt God can contrive matter so that there shall be other sort of proportions, that may be quite of a different kind, and may raise another sort of pleasure in the sense, and in a manner to us inconceivable, that shall be vastly more ravishing and exquisite. . . . Our animal spirits will also be capable of immensely more, fine and exquisite proportions in their motions than now they are, being so gross."[5]

I love it! Pleasures that are vastly more ravishing and exquisite. In a word, there are dimensions to physical reality and depths of spiritual apprehension and faculties of sensation and joy, of which we yet know nothing, that God will "contrive" in new, unforeseen, "immensely more, fine and exquisite proportions" to facilitate our eternal satisfaction in him.

Oh, blessed bread of life—glorify yourself by feeding me forever!

20

A New Name
Written Down in Glory

Revelation 2:17

"To the one who conquers I will give some of the hidden manna, and I will give him a white stone, with a new name written on the stone that no one knows except the one who receives it."

The white stone in Revelation 2:17, given to those who conquer, or overcome, has been subjected to as many differing interpretations as have the "two witnesses" of Revelation 11. That doesn't mean we are hopeless in our efforts to understand what Jesus meant, but it does suggest that we should be cautious and avoid dogmatism, regardless of whichever view we ultimately embrace.

Some argue that the white stone signified acquittal by a jury, as over against a black stone that pointed to the guilt of the defendant. If that is the background to our text, Jesus would be highlighting the reality of our forgiveness. What a blessed image indeed, that God the Father pronounces us not guilty by virtue of the redemptive work of his Son, our Savior.

Others point to the practice of certain pagan religions in which people would carry an amulet or stone with the name of their deity inscribed upon it. It supposedly was used as a source of magical power. If this is the background to our Lord's reference, "the written name will be that of God or of Christ, as in Rev[elation] 3:12 (cf.

14.1; 19.12). The point is then an allusion to ancient ideas of the power of divine names. To know the name of a deity was to possess a claim upon his help: here the power of Christ to save and protect is exalted over that of his pagan rivals."[6]

I could go on listing options, but let me come to the view that I think is most likely. White stones were often used as *tokens of membership or tickets for admission* to public festivals. If this is the background for the text, the white stone *may* be a symbol for the believer's admission to the messianic feast of Revelation 19. It is white in order to portray the righteousness of those who are granted entrance. As we read in Revelation 19:8, it was granted to the bride, i.e., the church, "'to clothe herself with fine linen, bright and pure'— for the fine linen is the righteous deeds of the saints."

Little wonder, then, that John goes on to write, "The angel said to me, 'Write this: Blessed are those who are invited to the marriage supper of the Lamb'" (Rev. 19:9a). Blessed indeed!

I must confess that I'm even more intrigued by the new name written on the stone "that no one knows except the one who receives it" (Rev. 2:17). This is clearly an allusion to the prophecy in Isaiah 62:2: "The nations shall see your righteousness, and all the kings your glory, and *you shall be called by a new name* that the mouth of the LORD will give"; and 65:15: "but his [God's] servants he will call by *another name.*" In both cases these concern Israel's future kingly status and restoration to Yahweh but are here applied to individuals within the church, she who is the true Israel of God.

Another question is whether this new name given to the over-comer is Christ's or the individual's. Greg Beale believes that the name in Revelation 2:17 is a reference to the "name of my God, and the name of the city of my God, the new Jerusalem, which comes down from my God out of heaven, and my [Christ's] new name" in Revelation 3:12. These are not separate names, notes Beale, but "all refer to the intimate eschatological presence of God and Christ with his people," as expressed most clearly by Revelation 22:3–4.[7]

That's certainly a possibility, but I'm inclined to think the "new name" in verse 17 is one given uniquely to each individual believer and that it "symbolizes the individual's entry into a new life, status or personality. . . . The thought may then be compared with that of 2 Cor. 5:17."[8] In other words, because those who are in Christ are now "new creations," it is only fitting that they should each receive a "new name" suitable to their position in and relationship with Jesus.

This isn't to say that the old or original name, given to us by our parents or the world, is evil or to be casually discarded. Rather, one's name, at least in biblical times, typically signified or pointed to one's character or calling or function. Today, we name our children for altogether different reasons. Perhaps we hope their name will inspire confidence and power, so we name a son Gregory rather than Gomer, with all due apologies to any of you whose name actually is Gomer, or a daughter Melissa rather than Minnie Ola. I can get away with that one since Minnie Ola was my grandmother's name.

Others select names based on what's fashionable or on what rhymes. Some, such as I, are named after grandparents or to reflect a biblical truth. *Charissa* comes from the Greek word for "grace," and *Sophia* from the Greek word for "wisdom," just to cite two examples. But in biblical days a person's name was more than simply a label to differentiate him or her from others. A person didn't simply have a name—a person *was* his name. Name ideally reflected nature.

All this to say that God will rename each of us in accordance with the transformation of our nature into the likeness of his Son, to reflect the new and altogether unique identity each has received by grace and the irrevocable destiny we have in Christ. My new name, like yours, will reflect the character of the new creation in which I am a participant, as over against the old or original creation corrupted by sin and death. My new name, like yours, will be suitable to the new heavens and new earth in which I'll dwell, a place devoid of evil and error.

But there is more to this new name than merely its newness. It is a name that no one knows except for the individual who receives it. Might this point to the intimate, intensely personal nature of one's life in God? Could it be that Jesus is highlighting the depths of intimacy and acceptance that each of us enjoys, and especially *will* enjoy, in the secret recesses of our souls? Yes, I think so.

In this regard we must also remember that the manna given to us is described as "hidden" (Rev. 2:17a). Some believe this is simply a reference to its having been hidden in a jar in the ark of the covenant, but I think something more is involved. If Jesus is himself the manna, perhaps the point is that all that awaits us in him is hidden in the sense that it is reserved and kept safe and guarded against all possibility of loss so that we might revel in its certainty and the assurance that what God has promised, he will indeed provide.

To sum up, there is an *identity* you have in God, reflected in your new name, that transcends whatever shame or regret or disappointment is wrapped up in who you are now. There is a very private and personal place of intimacy with him that brings hope and freedom and joy that none can touch or taint or steal away. Paul said it best when he declared that "your life is hidden with Christ in God" (Col. 3:3b). Peter echoed much the same thing in saying that we have "an inheritance that is imperishable, undefiled, and unfading, kept in heaven" for us (1 Pet. 1:4).

It's not the greatest hymn ever written, but I remember as a child singing "A New Name in Glory" by C. Austin Miles. The only line that stayed with me is found in the chorus: "There's a new name written down in glory, and it's mine, O yes, it's mine!" I don't yet know what it is, but I will! Praise God, I will.

Part 4

The Church in Thyatira

A nd to the angel of the church in Thyatira write: "The words of the Son of God, who has eyes like a flame of fire, and whose feet are like burnished bronze. I know your works, your love and faith and service and patient endurance, and that your latter works exceed the first. But I have this against you, that you tolerate that woman Jezebel, who calls herself a prophetess and is teaching and seducing my servants to practice sexual immorality and to eat food sacrificed to idols. I gave her time to repent, but she refuses to repent of her sexual immorality. Behold, I will throw her onto a sickbed, and those who commit adultery with her I will throw into great tribulation, unless they repent of her works, and I will strike her children dead. And all the churches will know that I am he who searches mind and heart, and I will give to each of you according to your works. But to the rest of you in Thyatira, who do not hold this teaching, who have not learned what some call the deep things of Satan, to you I say, I do not lay on you any other burden. Only hold fast what you have until I come. The one who conquers and who keeps my works until the end, to him I will give authority over the nations, and he will rule them with a rod of iron, as when earthen pots are broken in pieces, even as I myself have received authority from my Father. And I will give him the morning star. He who has an ear, let him hear what the Spirit says to the churches."

21

The Threat of Spiritual Inertia

Revelation 2:18–19

"And to the angel of the church in Thyatira write: 'The words of the Son of God, who has eyes like a flame of fire, and whose feet are like burnished bronze. I know your works, your love and faith and service and patient endurance, and that your latter works exceed the first.'"

Consider this challenge that I regularly put to myself and now put to you. Recall to mind the early days of your Christian life, perhaps the first year or so after your conversion. Do you remember the zeal for God and fascination with all things biblical you felt in the wake of saving grace? Think back on your evangelistic zeal and the courage you displayed in sharing your faith with unsaved family members and friends. Think back on the time and energy expended in service and prayer and ministry in the local church. Is it fresh in your mind? Got the picture?

Now, compare it with where you are today. Has your affection for God's people grown cold? Are you filled with doubts and fears rather than faith and confidence? Have you found excuses not to teach that Sunday school class or participate in the church choir? Do you find yourself rationalizing your absence from corporate worship or nurturing bitterness toward another believer who harmed you?

I'm the first to acknowledge that it's a challenge I'd rather not accept. It's painful and convicting to compare where I was with where I am, where I used to be with where I ought to be in my Christian growth.

Some who profess faith in Christ aren't in the least unnerved by this challenge. They're content with the spiritual status quo. In fact, the only thing that irritates them is being challenged to press on to greater conformity to Christ and more fervent love for his people. "Christianity is all about getting saved and escaping the horror of hell," so they say. "I'm happy where I am in life. Don't pressure me with a call to greater service. I've done my fair share of religious duties. My time card's been punched and I'd really like to be left alone to work on my golf game."

If that's an exaggeration of what professing Christians actually say, it's spot on target with how they actually live. They walked the aisle. They signed the card. They prayed the prayer. What more do you expect? Well, a lot more, actually.

The Christians who lived in ancient Thyatira would never have understood that mentality. In fact, it's the one thing for which Jesus praised them. Having been born again, they refused to coast. Their early diligence in ministry and mercy toward others had only increased with time. Hardship hadn't dimmed their faith. Familiarity with Christ had certainly not bred contempt. Here is what Jesus said to them: "And to the angel of the church in Thyatira write: 'The words of the Son of God, who has eyes like a flame of fire, and whose feet are like burnished bronze. I know your works, your love and faith and service and patient endurance, and that *your latter works exceed the first*" (Rev. 2:18–19). The emphasis is mine, but only because it is assuredly a point of emphasis from our Lord.

Thyatira was the least known, least remarkable, and least important of the seven cities to receive a letter from the Lord. Perhaps its only claim to fame was that Lydia had lived there (see Acts 16:11–15). Yet the letter addressed to it is the longest and most difficult to interpret. The obscurity of the letter and the enigmatic character of certain words and phrases are largely due to the fact that background information on the history of Thyatira, specifically the cultural conditions and circumstances in the first century, is almost wholly lacking. Its spiritual condition, on the other hand, is similar to that of Pergamum. Although they are commended for increase in growth and service, there is toleration of falsehood and moral compromise in their midst.

As noted, Thyatira was a comparatively unimportant city. It had no significant military, political, or administrative responsibilities, and if it is to be noted for anything, it is its commercial enterprises. It was a center for manufacturing and marketing and its most distinguishing characteristic was the large number of trade guilds that flourished there, the existence of which posed a special problem for Christians (to be noted later). One thing is clear: by the close of the first century the church in Thyatira was both prosperous and active.

The description of Jesus as one with "eyes like a flame of fire" and "feet . . . like burnished bronze" is probably an allusion to the fiery furnace of Daniel 3 into which Shadrach, Meshach, and Abednego were thrown. The added reference to Jesus as "the Son of God" (only here in Revelation, but 46 times in the New Testament) confirms this, for the three Jewish men were delivered by one "like a son of the gods" (Dan. 3:25).

The Thyatirans ought to be encouraged by this word of commendation. Among the deeds, or works, that Jesus knows are their "love and faith and service and patient endurance." But surely the best thing said of them is that their "latter works exceed the first." In other words, the church in Thyatira was a growing church, not so much numerically but in Christlike qualities. They had learned that the Christian life is one of growth, progress, development, and spiritual increase. Merely maintaining the moral status quo, whether individually or corporately, is inadequate.

Thus whereas Ephesus was backsliding, Thyatira was moving forward. I think we're justified, then, in adding this as another quality of the church that Jesus approves: to the doctrinal orthodoxy of Ephesus, the suffering for righteousness' sake of Smyrna, the love of Pergamum, we now add the growth and development of Thyatira.

That's a wonderful legacy, to be known as a church that has faithfully built on the original foundation of love, laboring in God's grace to fan that first flame into a full-blown forest fire of affection and devotion to one another. Not only that, but their faith had increased. Their knowledge of God and his ways and the confidence it breeds had deepened and expanded. But doctrine hadn't gone merely into their heads but had energized their hands as they grew in service and sacrifice for one another. And when times got tough, and the temptation to quit grew more alluring, they persevered.

Surprisingly, though, there was something missing. Some in Thyatira, clearly not all, as verse 24 makes clear, had grown tolerant of the "woman Jezebel" (v. 20) and her wicked ways. The fruit of this compromise had grown rotten and threatened the very life of the body as a whole. Christ simply won't have it, as we'll soon see.

But there is this to learn from the church in Thyatira: the Christian life is an ever-upward trek toward greater heights of holiness and love and theological understanding. Being born again is only a beginning, not an end; an inauguration, not a consummation. Appealing to one's initial zeal as an excuse for shifting into spiritual cruise-control won't set well with our Lord.

So, how'd you fare with the challenge? Are there signs of growth? Has love grown, or simply grown old and cold? Do the works of late exceed those first done?

"Lord, shatter our complacency. Disrupt our indifference. Move us off dead center. Overcome our spiritual inertia and lovingly lead us into new vistas of knowledge of you and love for your people and commitment to your kingdom! May we, by your grace, be people of whom it is said, 'your latter works exceed the first.' Amen."

22

That Woman, Jezebel

Revelation 2:20

"I have this against you, that you tolerate that woman Jezebel,
who calls herself a prophetess and is teaching and seducing my
servants to practice sexual immorality and to eat food sacrificed
to idols."

How tragic, after reading of the splendid qualities in Thyatira, to discover that moral compromise was present in the church. "I have this against you," said Jesus, "that you tolerate that woman Jezebel, who calls herself a prophetess and is teaching and seducing my servants to practice sexual immorality and to eat food sacrificed to idols" (Rev. 2:20).

John Stott put it bluntly: "In that fair field a poisonous weed was being allowed to luxuriate. In that healthy body a malignant cancer had begun to form. An enemy was being harboured in the midst of the fellowship."[1]

The similarity between Thyatira and Pergamum and their joint dissimilarity with Ephesus here comes to the fore. The Ephesians could not bear the presence of falsehood and took no uncertain steps in ridding the cancerous error from their assembly. But as noted earlier, it was done at the expense of love. Not so with Thyatira. While abounding in love they had lost their sensitivity to error and had compromised the glorious truths of both doctrinal and moral uprightness.

The exact nature of the heresy in Thyatira was wrapped up in the person and practices of this woman called Jezebel. Several suggestions have been made as to her identity.

Those who find in the seven letters a prophetic outline of the history of the church seek to identify the church of Thyatira with the Roman Catholic Church of the Middle Ages. John Walvoord, former President of Dallas Theological Seminary, had this to say:

> During this period [i.e., the Middle Ages] also there began that exaltation of Mary the mother of our Lord which has tended to exalt her to the plane of a female deity through whom intercession to God should be made, and apart from whose favor there can be no salvation. The prominence of a woman prophetess in the church at Thyatira anticipates the prominence of this unscriptural exaltation of Mary.[2]

Others have suggested that Jezebel is none other than Lydia herself, who, if it were true, had badly fallen from the initial spiritual heights that we read about in Acts 16. Of course, there is nothing at all in the biblical text to suggest this identification.

A few Greek manuscripts include the possessive pronoun *your*, on the basis of which it is argued that Jezebel was the wife of the senior pastor in Thyatira. But even if the pronoun is original, it probably references the corporate church in Thyatira since the preceding four uses of the singular *your* in verses 19–20 clearly do so.

Jezebel may be a veiled reference to the pagan prophetess Sibyl Sambathe, for whom a shrine had been built just outside the walls of the city. This is doubtful, however, and for two reasons: first, she is spoken of in rather definite terms, implying that a distinct historical personality is in mind and not merely a shrine to a pagan goddess; and second, the text suggests that the individual was actually a member of the church of Thyatira, externally, at any rate, and under the jurisdiction and authority of its leaders.

The most likely interpretation is that, in view of the opportunity granted to her for repentance, Jezebel was a female member of the church who was promoting destructive heresies and leading many into moral compromise.

She was a real person, but the name Jezebel is probably symbolic. (It's hard to imagine anyone deliberately naming their daughter

Jezebel!) Note the parallel in the letter to Pergamum in which the Nicolaitans are subsumed under the name of an Old Testament figure, Balaam. The name Jezebel had, in fact, become proverbial for wickedness. Thus, what is meant is that this disreputable, so-called prophetess was as wicked and dangerous an influence in Thyatira as Jezebel had been to Israel in the Old Testament.

Note also that she calls herself a prophetess (v. 20). I can't imagine Jesus using this language if her prophetic gift was of the Holy Spirit. Some contend she was a born-again believer who had simply gone astray, but I suggest that her behavior and beliefs are an indication that whatever claims she made to being saved and prophetically gifted were spurious. This isn't to say she didn't have a supernatural power, but the latter need not always be from God (see Matt. 7:21–23; Acts 16:16–18; 2 Thess. 2:9–10).

According to 1 Kings 16:31, the Old Testament Jezebel was the daughter of Ethbaal, king of the Sidonians, who married Ahab, king of Israel. Largely because of her influence in seeking to combine the worship of Yahweh with the worship of Baal, it is said of her husband that he "did more to provoke the LORD, the God of Israel, to anger than all the kings of Israel who were before him" (1 Kings 16:33).

Jezebel was responsible for the killing of Naboth and confiscation of his vineyard for her husband (1 Kings 21:1–6). She sought the death of all the prophets of Israel (1 Kings 18:4; 2 Kings 9) and even came close to killing Elijah (1 Kings 19:1-3). Her death came as a result of being thrown from a window where she was then trampled by a horse. When an attempt was made to recover her body for burial, it was discovered that the only thing left was her skull, her feet, and the palms of her hands. According to 2 Kings 9:36–37, dogs had eaten her flesh, in fulfillment of a prophetic word from Elijah:

> When they came back and told him, he said, "This is the word of the LORD, which he spoke by his servant Elijah the Tishbite, 'In the territory of Jezreel the dogs shall eat the flesh of Jezebel, and the corpse of Jezebel shall be as dung on the face of the field in the territory of Jezreel, so that no one can say, "This is Jezebel."'"

Although the first Jezebel had been dead for over one thousand years, her spirit had, as it were, found new life in this woman of Thyatira. She may even have been the leader or hostess of a house-church in the city. But what did she advocate that led to her being labeled with this horrid name? It's likely she had exploited the commercial prosperity of Thyatira to justify and subsidize her immorality and that of her followers. Leon Morris explains:

> The strong trade guilds in this city would have made it very difficult for any Christian to earn his living without belonging to a guild. But membership involved attendance at guild banquets, and this in turn meant eating meat which had first been sacrificed to an idol. . . . That these meals all too readily degenerated into sexual looseness made matters worse. But we can understand that some Christians would welcome a heresy of this type. It enabled them to maintain a Christian profession while countenancing and even engaging in immoral heathen revels.[3]

The complaint of the Lord lies in the unhealthy degree of toleration granted this woman. When it is said, "You tolerate that woman Jezebel," the implication is that the church in general did not accept her teaching nor adopt her lifestyle. But the subsequent mention of her lovers and children in verse 22 indicates that a number in the community did so. These would have formed a distinct group within the church, and the church as a whole was content for them to remain.

Whereas it is probable that one individual woman is in view, others have suggested that the reference to "the woman" and "her children" sounds strangely similar to the phrase "the elect lady and her children" in 2 John 1. In 2 John this refers to the church community as a whole and to the individuals who are each a part of it. Perhaps, then, "Jezebel" is not a single person but a collective reference to a group of false prophets and prophetesses in Thyatira.

Whether one or many, the presence of such a corrosive and corrupting influence in the church, in *any* church, simply cannot be allowed. To be continued . . .

23

Jezebel and Her Children

Revelation 2:21–23a

"I gave her time to repent, but she refuses to repent of her sexual immorality. Behold, I will throw her onto a sickbed, and those who commit adultery with her I will throw into great tribulation, unless they repent of her works, and I will strike her children dead."

I'm constantly stunned by the gracious and longsuffering character of our Lord Jesus Christ. Listen to his words in the letter to the church at Thyatira: "*I gave her time to repent,* but she refuses to repent of her sexual immorality. Behold, I will throw her onto a sickbed, and those who commit adultery with her I will throw into great tribulation, unless they repent of her works, and I will strike her children dead" (Rev. 2:21–23a).

What a stunning display of kindness and mercy, that this woman who so horribly perverted the grace of God and used it as an excuse for idolatry and licentiousness should receive the extended opportunity to turn from her ways and receive the salvation of God! By all counts she should have been immediately cast into eternal darkness. But, then, so should all of us. Praise God for his blessed longsuffering.

But our Lord's patience has its limits. He will not indulge sin forever. He is no less holy and just than he is good and gracious.

Jezebel obviously presumed on God's grace and interpreted his longsuffering as approval or endorsement of her sinful ways, or at least his indifference toward her chosen paths. There may have been a definite time in the past when through some means, whether a prophetic word or direct encounter or perhaps through John, he issued this woman a warning, no doubt repeatedly. Whatever the case, the culpability of the false prophetess is evident. She refuses to repent. She clearly knew what was at issue and chose voluntarily to remain in her sin.

This raises an important theological and practical question: was Jezebel a Christian? My earlier comments would indicate I believe her to be unsaved, and thus some may react in horror that I raise the possibility that she might be born again. On first glance, the nature of her sin and her refusal to repent point to an unregenerate heart. But there are other factors to be considered.

For example, her judgment is said to come in the form of personal sickness, disease, or physical affliction of some sort. Jesus says, "I will throw her onto a sickbed," language that is reminiscent of the discipline imposed on the *Christians* at Corinth who had persistently abused the Eucharist (see 1 Cor. 11:30–32). And before we too quickly conclude that someone born again could not commit such sins as are described in this passage, we should note that she is specifically charged with "teaching and seducing *my servants* to practice sexual immorality and to eat food sacrificed to idols" (v. 20). Note well: those whom Jesus calls "my servants" are guilty of sexual immorality and eating food sacrificed to idols.

Of those who participate with her in these sins, Jesus says, "I will strike her children dead." The text could literally be translated, "I will kill with death," a proverbial statement that means "to slay utterly." Although this sounds more severe than what we might call divine discipline of a wayward believer, is it so different from how God dealt with Ananias and Sapphira in Acts 5?

The fact that they are called her children does not mean they are the actual physical progeny of her many sexual infidelities. They are, rather, "those who have so unreservedly embraced the antinomian doctrines of their spiritual mother that they are best described as younger members of her family."[4] In other words, those who commit adultery with her (v. 22) and her children (v. 23) are the same people.

This also raises, yet again, the question of whether or not the sexual immorality in view is literal and physical or a metaphor of

114

spiritual unfaithfulness and idolatry, perhaps especially manifest in unhealthy and illicit compromise with pagan culture. The evidence is mixed. On the one hand, I can't dismiss the possibility that literal sexual promiscuity is involved. After all, it is rare for one to embrace idolatry without yielding to sexual temptation. See especially Romans 1:18ff. So perhaps, in the final analysis, it is a false dichotomy to insist that she be guilty of *either* sexual immorality *or* religious idolatry. They seem so often (always?) to go hand in hand.

On the other hand, since there were surely at least some female followers of Jezebel, the adultery they are said to have committed with her would likely, at least in their case, be metaphorical for spiritual infidelity.

Jesus says they must repent of "her" works, i.e., since they have joined with her in this sin, to repent of what she did is to repent of what they, too, did. If they do not, Jesus will throw them into great tribulation. The precise nature of this tribulation is not specified, but it would surely involve, at minimum, physical illness that in the absence of repentance would culminate in physical death.

Let me bring this to a close with two observations.

First, although I can't be dogmatic about it, I'm inclined to think that Jezebel was an unbeliever. The fact that she is designated by a name that is linked historically to a woman of almost unimaginable wickedness and perversity suggests that she, too, is utterly unregenerate and devoid of spiritual life. But I could be wrong on this.

Second, having said that, I must also say, reluctantly, that Christians *can* fall into grievous and horrific sin. As noted, Jesus here says that his "servants" have joined with Jezebel in her works. The divine response of our heavenly Father to his backslidden children isn't eternal judgment but firm and loving discipline (see especially Hebrews 12). If that discipline is not met with heartfelt repentance, it may well lead to physical (not spiritual) death. This was certainly the case with Ananias and Sapphira (Acts 5) as well as the believers in Corinth. It would appear also to be the case with some of those in the church at Thyatira.

These are difficult matters that cannot be ignored, treated casually, or dismissed with cavalier dogmatism. Having said that, I am confident of two things. First, our Lord *will* deal with unrepentant sin. He himself declares in verse 23, "I will give to each of you according to your works." It may not happen immediately, longsuffering as he is, but in the absence of heartfelt conviction and repentance, it will most assuredly happen. Second, although we may not have the discernment to know infallibly who is and is not saved, "the Lord knows those who are his" (2 Tim. 2:19).

24

He Knows Our Kidneys

Revelation 2:23

"Behold, I will throw her onto a sickbed, and those who commit adultery with her I will throw into great tribulation, unless they repent of her works, and I will strike her children dead. **And all the churches will know that I am he who searches mind and heart, and I will give to each of you as your works deserve.**"

Our Lord clearly states that the casting of Jezebel on a sickbed and the infliction of her children with great tribulation, to the point of physical death itself, will be an unmistakable sign to all that nothing escapes his gaze or slips in beneath the radar, so to speak. But how does Christ's judgment against the unrepentant reveal to all Christians everywhere that he has exhaustive and altogether accurate knowledge of the hearts and minds of everyone?

Look again at Revelation 2:23. Following his declaration of impending discipline, he says, "All the churches will know that I am he who searches mind and heart, and I will give to each of you as your works deserve."

Before we consider this issue I want to make clear how loudly this passage shouts, "Jesus Christ is God!" We see it in verse 23 in two ways. First, he is *omniscient*, a recurring theme throughout these letters to the churches. The statement here is an obvious allusion to verse 18 where he is described as the one who "has eyes like a flame of fire." His gaze penetrates all human pretense. His searing vision yields to no barrier. Try as we may to obscure his sight or distract his focus, our Lord sees through and beyond every human façade, every evasive tactic, every clever cover-up.

But there is a second way in which our Lord's deity is seen. Revelation 2:23 is an unmistakable allusion to Jeremiah 17:10, where we read, "I the LORD search the heart and test the mind [lit., "kidneys" in Hebrew], to give every man according to his ways, according to the fruit of his deeds."

The significance of this latter text is that it is Yahweh who is speaking of himself. Yet here in Revelation it is a description of Jesus. Jesus *is* Yahweh incarnate. He is not only omniscient Deity; he is also the Judge of all mankind. He sees and knows all and will call all to account for their deeds.

Let's return now to the issue at hand. Jesus declares that his decisive action against unrepentant sinners in Thyatira is a warning to all. It should forever put to rest any lingering doubts about whether he knows what is going on in his churches and whether he is of the inclination to take whatever steps are necessary to rectify matters when they get out of hand.

By observing what befalls those in Thyatira, Christians in other congregations will immediately know that Jesus knew and that he will hold all accountable for their deeds. There's no miscarriage of justice here. No legal sleight of hand. No such thing as inadmissible evidence or testimony being stricken from the record. The judgment of Jesus is based on comprehensive knowledge of every idea in the mind and every impulse of the heart of all mankind.

The word translated "mind" is literally the word for "kidneys" (*nephros*). It was often used to describe the inmost, secretive, solemn movements of the soul. Those deep inner impulses we so naïvely think are hidden from everyone but ourselves are seen with utmost clarity by the Lord Jesus. Every intent of the heart, every meditation of the mind, every fantasy, fear, emotion, doubt, deliberation, and decision are the focus of his penetrating gaze.

That is why we can rest assured that those who suffer, as did those in Thyatira, are not mistreated. The disciplinary hand of God is guided by the comprehensive scope of his understanding. No one can protest by saying, "But God, that's not what I *truly* meant," or

"But God, I *actually* intended to do otherwise," for God knows every purpose, plan, and premeditation.

Every affection is seen for what it is, no matter how hard we may strive to conceal it within. Every attitude is known for what it entails, notwithstanding our most diligent efforts to convince ourselves and others that we never entertained such thoughts or conceived such fantasies.

No one expressed it more clearly than the apostle Paul, whose language in 1 Corinthians 4:3–5 veritably echoes that of Jesus in Revelation 2. I'll close with his words:

> But with me it is a very small thing that I should be judged by you or by any human court. In fact, I do not even judge myself. For I am not aware of anything against myself, but I am not thereby acquitted. It is the Lord who judges me. Therefore do not pronounce judgment before the time, before the Lord comes, who will bring to light the things now hidden in darkness and will disclose the purposes of the heart. Then each one will receive his commendation from God.

25

The "Jezebel Spirit"

Revelation 2:20–23

"But I have this against you, that you tolerate that woman Jezebel, who calls herself a prophetess and is teaching and seducing my servants to practice sexual immorality and to eat food sacrificed to idols. I gave her time to repent, but she refuses to repent of her sexual immorality. Behold, I will throw her onto a sickbed, and those who commit adultery with her I will throw into great tribulation, unless they repent of her works, and I will strike her children dead. And all the churches will know that I am he who searches mind and heart, and I will give to each of you according to your works."

How is it that this woman called Jezebel came to exert such incredible power over the lives of Christians in Thyatira? What accounts for the authority she possessed to convince the followers of Jesus to abandon their commitment to ethical purity and engage in sexual immorality and other forms of compromise with the surrounding culture?

There's no indication that she held an ecclesiastical office. She wasn't an elder or pastor or apostle. But she did claim to possess the gift of prophecy. Jesus said she "calls herself a prophetess" (v. 20).

Some may be tempted to dismiss Jezebel's claim based on their belief that women are not allowed to exercise this spiritual gift. A quick look at several texts from the New Testament will demonstrate that women did indeed prophesy under the influence of the Holy

Spirit. That doesn't mean Jezebel did, but her gender was itself no barrier to the proper exercise of this gift.

In Peter's speech on the day of Pentecost he explicitly said that characteristic of the present church age is the Spirit's impartation to *both men and women* of the prophetic gift. Look closely at his citation of Joel's promise: "And in the last days it shall be, God declares, that I will pour out my Spirit on all flesh, and your sons and your *daughters* shall prophesy, and your young men shall see visions, and your old men shall dream dreams; even on my male servants and *female* servants in those days I will pour out my Spirit, and they shall prophesy" (Acts 2:17–18).

In Acts 21:9 Luke refers to the four daughters of Philip as having the gift of prophecy. And in 1 Corinthians 11:5 Paul gave instructions regarding how women were to pray and prophesy in the church meeting.[5]

Is Jesus suggesting she only claimed to have this gift but in fact did not? Or did she have a genuine spiritual gift but abused it in ways inconsistent with New Testament guidelines on how it was to be exercised? If Jezebel was not a Christian, as I have argued, it is most likely that she exercised a supernatural prophetic-like ability that was energized by demonic power rather than the Spirit of God. That this was (and is) distinctly possible is evident from Matthew 7:21–23, Acts 16:16–18, and perhaps 2 Thessalonians 2:9–10.

It's not out of the question that the presence of such false prophets and the havoc they wreaked in the early church was the principal reason why some in Thessalonica had grown weary of this phenomenon and had begun to "despise" all prophetic utterances (1 Thess. 5:20), even those that clearly were prompted by the Spirit. Paul's exhortation is that they not allow the damage perpetrated by the spurious to undermine the benefits that accrue from the genuine.

I want to suggest that it was possibly (probably?) through this alleged prophetic ability that Jezebel gained power and authority in the church at Thyatira and adversely influenced a number of Christians there. It's not difficult to see how this could and does occur. By the way, a man can display the characteristics of Jezebel no less than a woman. This is one sin that is by no means gender specific.

A brief word is in order about my use of the phrase "spirit of Jezebel" or "Jezebel spirit," language that, although not strictly biblical, has been bandied about in charismatic circles for generations, but perhaps is not as familiar to those in mainstream evangelicalism. I've read numerous articles and books and listened to an equal number of sermons on the so-called Jezebel spirit. To be honest, I haven't found them very helpful. In most cases they are speculative meanderings that show little concern for the biblical text.

Let me be brief and simply say that the word *spirit* is used here in one of two ways: either (1) of the *human* spirit, perhaps an attitude, disposition, habit, or set of characteristics displayed by a particular individual; or (2) of those whose supernatural prophetic ability is energized by a *demonic* spirit. In either case, regardless of the animating force, a person with a "Jezebel spirit" is one who displays the insidious, manipulative, and evil tendencies manifest in this woman of Thyatira.

So what kind of person do I have in mind, and what is it that they do? All too often we hear of individuals using their ecclesiastical authority or position as well as their supernatural gifting, whether it be of God or the enemy, to manipulate others into behavior they would not normally embrace. I'm burdened by the number of instances in which even Christians who are prophetically gifted use their endowment to expand their sphere of influence for personal profit or are afforded unwarranted privileges in the local church.

Virtually everyone is aware of some situation in which a Christian has used a spiritual gift, whether teaching, administration, pastoring, or another of the *charismata* to gain illicit control and influence within the wider body of Christ. So it should come as no surprise that someone who legitimately possesses the gift of prophecy might abuse it to enhance their status or broaden their liberties or even seek monetary gain.

The most heinous abuse of a prophetic gift is when appeal is made to special revelatory insights in order to justify immorality or, at minimum, to ignore it. Similarly, because of the "wonderful contribution" that a person has made to the kingdom, he or she is virtually untouchable and rarely held accountable to the normal rules of ethical behavior that govern all other Christians. Anyone who "hears" God with such regularity and alleged accuracy, so they contend, is unique, extraordinarily anointed, and therefore so highly favored of God that they needn't worry about the temptations that average Christians face or the tendencies of the flesh against which we typically wage war on a daily basis.

On occasion, a person with a Jezebel spirit will claim to have revelation that trumps Scripture, although they would rarely, if ever, put it in such stark terms; a person with this "spirit" is subtle, if nothing. Because such "words" from God are direct and immediate, and can't be explained by appeal to what one knows by natural means, they are falsely perceived as carrying greater authority than the inspired text itself. Or it is revelation that allegedly provides a superior and formerly unknown interpretation of Scripture that makes it possible to circumvent or at least treat with casual disdain the Bible's doctrinal precepts and ethical commands.

A person with a "Jezebel spirit" is one who appeals to his or her "spirituality" to rationalize, or again, at minimum, to overlook sensuality. Often they don't even believe it to be sinful or illicit but are so blinded by pride, the praise of men, and sensational supernatural experiences that what may well be inappropriate for mainstream believers is, in their case, permissible. It's just one of the perks.

Religious prestige is thus employed to foster sexual liberty. Under the pretense of anointed "ministry" a person exploits his or her platform and power to gain sexual favors or to lead others into similar behavior. This person is generally unaccountable to the leadership of the church, believing that the pastor and elders are unanointed or insufficiently gifted to appreciate the level of supernatural spirituality at which he or she operates on a daily basis.

Eventually a double standard emerges: one set of strict, biblical guidelines to govern ordinary Christians and the exercise of their gifts within the body, and a lax, minimal, or more flexible list of expectations by which the man or woman of God is to live. Needless to say, it's a prescription for moral disaster.

Make no mistake, the Jezebel who lived in Thyatira undoubtedly appealed to her prophetic gift and anointing to excuse her sexual immorality. She was using her power to manipulate others into sensuality and idolatry.

You may wonder why anyone would yield to such obvious unbiblical counsel, no matter how gifted the individual might be. It's not that difficult to understand. Some of you may be unaware of how mesmerizing and enticing the prospect of supernatural activity can be. When one witnesses what one believes is a genuine supernatural or miraculous event, otherwise normal theological defense mechanisms often fail to operate. Discernment is cast aside, lest it be viewed as a critical spirit or the response of a cynic. No one wants to be perceived as stiff-necked and resistant to the voice of God or the manifestation of his power. So, it is hard for some to resist and challenge the ministry of a recognized or alleged prophet in the church.

The spirit of Jezebel was not unique to the church in Thyatira. It is alive and well in the body of Christ today. One need only read the latest headlines. It is an insidious, yet subtle, spirit. It is destructive, yet enticing. It typically gains momentum among those who are so fearful of quenching the Spirit (1 Thess. 5:19) that they fail to rein in the flesh.

The solution is not to repudiate the prophetic altogether, or any other spiritual gift for that matter. Rather, we must become good Bereans, "examining the Scriptures daily" (Acts 17:11) to see if these things are of God or not. In sum, we would do well to heed Paul's counsel: "Do not despise prophecies, but test everything; hold fast what is good. Abstain from every form of evil" (1 Thess. 5:20–22).

26

Spiritual Osteoporosis

Revelation 2:24–25

"To the rest of you in Thyatira, who do not hold this teaching, who have not learned what some call the deep things of Satan, to you I say, I do not lay on you any other burden. Only hold fast what you have until I come."

Much of the church today is suffering from an advanced case of what I call *spiritual osteoporosis*. It's not widespread throughout the body of Christ but is concentrated along the spine. What I have in mind is the church's loss of its theological backbone.

We see this in any number of ways. For example, some have begun to fudge on the ethical status of homosexuality. Fearful of being labeled homophobic, they've adopted a "live and let live" approach to the issue. Others, not wanting to appear elitist or exclusivistic, no longer insist on personal faith in Christ as essential for salvation. Then there are those who've gone soft on the very concept of doctrine itself, believing that theological orthodoxy is both elusive and divisive and should be minimized for the sake of some ethereal and ill-defined unity.

I'm certainly no fan of angry sectarianism or the sort of dogmatic arrogance that judges and separates over secondary issues. At the same time, there *are* standards of truth to uphold and principles of behavior on which we must insist.

It's good to know that, notwithstanding the problems in ancient Thyatira, there were some in the church who refused to compromise or cut corners. Jesus describes them and delivers a special word of encouragement in verses 24–25 of Revelation 2: "But to the rest of you in Thyatira, who do not hold this teaching, who have not learned what some call the deep things of Satan, to you I say, I do not lay on you any other burden. Only hold fast what you have until I come."

There are four things here worthy of our attention. First, they are described as those "who do not hold this teaching," i.e., the teaching of Jezebel. Not only do they not embrace the doctrines she espouses but neither do they practice her wicked ways.

In other words, these are folks who refused to take the easy path by looking the other way. They were neither gullible nor easily persuaded by the novel and deceptive concepts circulating in Thyatira. These were people who weren't afraid of calling heresy *heresy*! The men and women Jesus addresses here knew that sometimes discrimination can be a virtue. They believed in the existence of absolute truth and unyielding ethical principles and were prepared to identify deviations from it. These were people who refused to embrace theological relativism, as if what one believes is less important than the sincerity and fervency with which one believes it.

Second, they are described as those "who have not learned what some call the deep things of Satan." This intriguing phrase calls for explanation. Some believe it to be a sarcastic reversal of the claims of Jezebel and "her children." They claim to know "deep [spiritual] things" when in fact what they know comes from and concerns the devil himself. In other words, the phrase "of Satan" is a sarcastic addition by Jesus designed to tell the faithful in Thyatira the true nature of their ideas and experience. Those of Jezebel may actually have used the words "of God" when making their claims, which Jesus deliberately alters to make the point.

Others suggest that the "deep things of Satan" is a reference to their insistence that in order to appreciate fully the depths of grace and of God (cf. 1 Cor. 2:10) one must first plumb the depths of evil and the enemy. They would claim that, because of their spiritual maturity and superiority, they need fear nothing from the devil.

On the other hand, the phrase "what some call" might be an instance in which the third-person plural is used without a subject to express an impersonal idea. Thus the phrase, "as they say" (literally translated), would not refer to anyone involved in the conflict at Thyatira but would merely convey an impersonal passive idea—"the deep things of Satan, *as it is said* by many," the "deep things" referring to a well-known expression for such teaching which Jesus picks up to describe the situation in Thyatira.

In any case, it's stunning to realize that people who profess to know Christ and attain to positions of authority and influence in the church can be proponents of satanic doctrine and practitioners of ethical compromise. What we desperately need today, as they did then, is an increase of (back)bone density, a strengthening of resolve to hold fast the line of orthodoxy, and a courageous commitment to that holiness of life that will assuredly evoke disdainful accusations of being narrow-minded and puritanical.

Third, Jesus obviously knew that what he expected of them wasn't easy. It called for sacrifice and diligent attentiveness to belief and behavior, the sort that would expose them to ridicule and perhaps loss of income and influence. Thus he says, "I do not lay on you any other burden." It is enough, says Jesus, that you stand firm. It is enough that you not lose heart. It is enough that you resist every temptation to cater to popular opinion or adjust your convictions to whatever theological trend is emerging in your city.

Fourth, and finally, he encourages them to hold fast what they have until he comes. In a word, *persevere* in what you have already received. Be immovable. Don't yield an inch. Cut not a corner!

All too often, especially in charismatic circles, the penchant for novelty or the hankering after some fresh word from God dictates the ministry or mission of a church. The frequency with which a pastor or teacher offers heretofore unknown insights into Scripture is made the measure of his anointing and favor with God. I'm not saying there is nothing more to learn from the Bible than what we now know. Far from it! But we must be careful lest the allure of newness detract us from focusing on the "old, old story of Jesus and his love" (I fear that few will recall that hymn).

By the way, lest you think that progress and improvement are incompatible with perseverance and stability, compare Revelation 2:19 with 2:25.

As for my concern with spiritual osteoporosis in the church today, I have no desire to see it replaced by a hardening of the theological arteries! Speaking the truth in love is never easy. But we must never play off one against the other. Jesus believed both were possible. So must we.

27

Was Jesus an Amillennialist?

Revelation 2:26–29

"The one who conquers and who keeps my works until the end, to him I will give authority over the nations, and he will rule them with a rod of iron, as when earthen pots are broken in pieces, even as I myself have received authority from my Father. And I will give him the morning star. He who has an ear, let him hear what the Spirit says to the churches."

Was Jesus an amillennialist? I know that's a provocative question, perhaps even incendiary to some of you. But let's look closely at the promised reward in this letter to the church in Thyatira. Those who overcome or conquer are the very people who are persecuted, thrown in prison, and even subjected to martyrdom (see Rev. 2:3, 9–11,13). The promise to them is that if they keep Christ's works until the end they will be given authority to rule over nations, even as Christ has been given authority from his Father to rule (see Psalm 2).

Who or what are these nations and when is it that Christians will exercise their rule over them? Some, perhaps most, believe this is a promise to be fulfilled on the millennial earth, that one-thousand-year period of human history that premillennialists believe will follow the second coming of Christ and precede the inauguration of the eternal state.

Bear with me as I make an alternative suggestion. Could it be that the reward noted here is the authority granted to the saints when they enter into co-regency with Christ in heaven *now*? A similar promise is made to the faithful in Laodicea: "The one who conquers, *I will grant him to sit with me on my throne* [namely, the place of rule, government, and authority], as I also conquered and sat down with my Father on his throne" (Rev. 3:21).

My point is that this co-regency with Christ is fulfilled now, in heaven, that is to say, in the so-called intermediate state where the dead in Christ live in conscious, intimate fellowship with the Savior. This co-regency, as I have called it, is therefore the same as the coming to life and reigning with Christ described in Revelation 20:4 and 20:6. The millennium or thousand-year rule is currently in session, as Christ, together with the overcomers or conquerors, rules with authority over the nations of the earth.

To put it simply and to the point: The conquerors or overcomers are not merely those over whom Christ *will* rule but those with whom Christ *now* rules.

We often fail to grasp the glory of what awaits those who die in the Lord and enter his presence. Although it is an intermediate state, that is to say, it is in between our present earthly existence and our final and glorified experience when we receive the resurrection body, it is nevertheless a wonderful and joyful and meaningful time. It is during this time, simultaneous with the present church age, that those who have died in Christ experience the fulfillment of this promise: they are even now ruling and reigning over the nations of the earth in tandem with their sovereign Lord.

For those of you not familiar with the debate over biblical eschatology, this is the perspective known as *amillennialism*. Contrary to the label that suggests we don't believe in the existence or reality of a millennium (observe how the alpha privative "a" seemingly negates the word *millennial*), we most assuredly do! The millennium is concurrent with the church age in which we live.

Again, contrary to the charge of spiritualizing the millennial kingdom, the saints truly and literally are enthroned with Christ; they are truly and literally reigning with Christ. This is not a metaphor, but a concrete and living reality. The millennium, therefore, isn't the experience of Christians in the church on earth but that of the saints in heaven. They have been enthroned. They now rule. They share in the exercise of Christ's dominion and sovereignty over the affairs and events and nations of the earth.

The apostle Paul had this in view in 1 Corinthians 15:24–26. There he describes Christ's current sovereign rule over the affairs of both heaven and earth, one in which, Jesus says here in Revelation 2:25–29, his people who conquer will share. Look at Paul's words to the Corinthians closely:

> Then comes the end, when he delivers the kingdom to God the Father after destroying every rule and every authority and power. For he must reign until he has put all his enemies under his feet. The last enemy to be destroyed is death.

Practically speaking, this means that Ignatius and Augustine, as well as Anselm and Aquinas, Calvin and Luther, Edwards and Wesley, Owen and Whitefield, together with Mary Magdalene, Aimee Semple McPherson, Susannah Wesley, and the untold millions of others who are "away from the body and at home with the Lord" (2 Cor. 5:1–10) are now exercising a divinely delegated authority in the providential oversight of the nations of the earth.

This enthronement and rule of the saints in heaven, with Christ, will continue far beyond the millennial phase in which it currently exists. There is an eternal expression of this experience that will unfold not only in the new heaven but also on the new earth (cf. Rev. 5:10) that will be created at the coming of Christ (Revelation 21–22). The nature of that authority and rule will undoubtedly change, given the fact that all unbelievers will have by then been banished to their eternal punishment in hell, but our co-regency with Christ will never cease.

As I read further in the passage before us now, Revelation 2:26–29, it appears that the promise of co-regency with Christ is reinforced yet again. In verse 28 Jesus declares that the overcomer will receive "the morning star." It's possible that this is a reference to Jesus himself (see Rev. 22:16). But there is another option that relates this statement to what has preceded in the immediate context. The morning star is generally regarded as referring to Venus, although it is technically a planet, which itself was an ancient symbol for sovereignty. In Roman times, notes Beasley-Murray, it was more specifically the symbol of victory and sovereignty, for which reason Roman generals owned their loyalty to Venus by erecting temples in her honour . . . and Caesar's legions carried her sign on their standards. . . . If then the morning star was the sign of conquest and rule over the nations, this element in the promise to the conqueror strengthens the statement that has gone before. It embodies in symbol the prophecy already cited from the psalmist. The conqueror is therefore doubly assured of his participation with Christ in the glory of his kingdom.[6]

I certainly have no illusions about resolving the often acrimonious debate over biblical eschatology. In fact, I suspect my comments in this meditation will provoke no little response, perhaps most of it negative. But as I read this passage, in conjunction with the whole of Scripture, I see a glorious affirmation of the destiny of the faithful who die in Christ.

To all outward appearances and the judgment of the unbelieving eye, it may seem that we have suffered loss. Yet, for the believer, to die is to live. What strikes the world as defeat and humiliation is for the Christian an entrance into life and exaltation. Let us never forget that the saints have conquered Satan "by the blood of the Lamb and by the word of their testimony, for they loved not their lives even unto death" (Rev. 12:11; see also Rev. 15:2; 17:14.).

So, was Jesus an amillennialist? Yes, I believe he was, and is.

Part 5

The Church in Sardis

And to the angel of the church in Sardis write: "The words of him who has the seven spirits of God and the seven stars. I know your works. You have the reputation of being alive, but you are dead. Wake up, and strengthen what remains and is about to die, for I have not found your works complete in the sight of my God. Remember, then, what you received and heard. Keep it, and repent. If you will not wake up, I will come like a thief, and you will not know at what hour I will come against you. Yet you have still a few names in Sardis, people who have not soiled their garments, and they will walk with me in white, for they are worthy. The one who conquers will be clothed thus in white garments, and I will never blot his name out of the book of life. I will confess his name before my Father and before his angels. He who has an ear, let him hear what the Spirit says to the churches."

28

Seeing Isn't Always Believing

Revelation 3:1

"I know your works. You have the reputation of being alive, but you are dead. Wake up, and strengthen what remains and is about to die, for I have not found your works complete in the sight of my God."

One of the more important lessons I've learned through the years, especially when it comes to church life, is that seeing isn't always believing. I don't want to sound cynical or pessimistic, but you shouldn't always trust your eyes. What I'm trying to say is that I'm not as impressed as I used to be when I hear of a church with a surging membership, multimillion-dollar budget, expansive facilities, and a reputation for programs, ministries, and a growing influence in the community.

The problem I have in mind isn't restricted to the so-called megachurch; it's just more conspicuous in their case. Even small congregations can be widely known for countless religious activities yet devoid of authentic commitment to Christ as Lord.

I typically read the Saturday edition of the *Kansas City Star* because it devotes a section to spiritual life in our city, with several pages listing the variety of churches and what each is offering during the week and especially on Sunday. Some of the ads look like a promo for the Ringling Brothers, Barnum & Bailey Circus. They've got gimmicks, gadgets, celebrity guest speakers and goodies of all sorts, most of which are designed to sell you an image of being alive and worthy of your attendance and your money, of course.

The church in first-century Sardis was just such a congregation. Let me illustrate. Try to envision the scene at a typical funeral with its sprays of flowers, and bright, vivid colors, all of which are designed, at least in part, to divert one's attention from the dark reality of death. The church at Sardis was like a beautifully adorned corpse in a funeral home, elegantly decked out in the visible splendor and fragrance of the most exquisite floral arrangement, set against the background of exquisite drapery and soft but uplifting music. Yet beneath the outward façade was death and spiritual putrefaction of the vilest sort. I don't recall who said or wrote it, but here is one pastor's exhortation to his own church to avoid the errors of Sardis:

> Ecclesiastical corpses lie all about us. The caskets in which they repose are lined with satin and are decorated with solid silver handles and abundant flowers. Like the other caskets, they are just large enough for their occupants with no room for converts. These churches have died of respectability and have been embalmed in self-complacency. If by the grace of God this church is alive, be warned to our opportunity or the feet of them that buried thy sister (Sardis) will be at the door to carry thee out too.

"Sardis," writes Beasley-Murray, "was a city of past glories. Once the capital of the ancient Lydian kingdom, it reached its pinnacle of fame under Croesus in the sixth century B.C., flourished under its Persian conquerors, but then went into an unceasing decline to obscurity."[1] This decline of the once great Sardis was aggravated by a devastating earthquake in A.D. 17, described by Pliny early in the second century as the greatest disaster in human memory, and despite the generous aid granted by the emperor Tiberius, "no city in Asia presented a more deplorable contrast of past splendour and present unresting decline."[2]

It would almost seem as though the history of the city was being relived in the church in its midst. Two specific elements in the city's life seem to find application in the letter to the church. Sardis was built on a mountain, and an acropolis was constructed on a spur of this mountain, which was all but impregnable. "To capture the acropolis of Sardis" had become proverbial for doing the impossible. Yet twice in the city's past it had been taken by surprise and captured by enemies. The parallel with the church's lack of vigilance, and its need to awaken lest it come under judgment (v. 3), is striking.

Furthermore, Sardis was also a great commercial center for woolen goods and claimed to be first in the field in the art of dyeing wool. This, too, appears to be reflected in verses 4–5 and may well have inspired the imagery employed there. Thus, "like the city itself," remarks Charles, "the church had belied its early promise. Its religious history, like its civil, belonged to the past."[3]

It comes as no great shock, then, when we discover that the letter our Lord addressed to the church in Sardis is one of the most severe of the seven. It is, in point of fact, along with the letter to Laodicea, the only church for which the Lord has no words of commendation. Simply put, *Jesus had nothing good to say about the church in Sardis.*

This letter stands out in sharp contrast to the four which have preceded it. To Ephesus, Smyrna, Pergamum, and Thyatira our Lord sends his greetings followed by a word of encouragement and praise. Their faults, be they ever so reprehensible, do appear to be exceptions to the general spirit of obedience and growth. But in Sardis there is no word of praise; obedience and growth, at best, are the exception, not the rule. Furthermore, we note that although Sardis is similar to Pergamum and Thyatira in that they all have mixed membership, in the latter two churches the faulty members are in the minority, but at Sardis they predominate. In Sardis only a "few names . . . have not soiled their garments" (v. 4). The majority had incurred defilement.

We might also ask why both Jews and Romans apparently left this church untouched when they so vigorously persecuted their neighbors. The answer may be its lack of spiritual integrity and whole-souled devotion to Christ. As Caird notes, "Content with mediocrity, lacking both the enthusiasm to entertain a heresy and the depth of conviction which provokes intolerance, it was too innocuous to be worth persecuting."[4] Simply put, *Sardis was the classic embodiment of inoffensive Christianity.*

The church in Sardis had acquired a reputation (v. 1b) in Asia Minor as a superlative congregation. To all external appearances, as far as what could be seen and heard, Sardis was a progressive church, first among its sister congregations to initiate a new program, full of vitality, overflowing with zeal, no doubt quite large. As you read John Stott's description of the church in Sardis, ask yourself whether it applies today. The answer could be painful.

> [Sardis] was positively humming with activity. There was no short-age in the church of money or talent or manpower. There was every indication of life and vigor. . . . But outward appearances are notori-ously deceptive; and this socially distinguished congregation was a spiritual graveyard. It seemed to be alive, but it was actually dead. It had a name for virility, but it had no right to its name. Its works were beautiful grave clothes which were but a thin disguise for this ecclesiastical corpse. The eyes of Christ saw beyond the clothes to the skeleton. It was dead as mutton. It even stank.[5]

There are numerous mega-churches, mini-churches, and every-thing in between that are not only outwardly active but also inwardly vibrant, genuine, and Christ-exalting in every way. We should thank God for them.

But there are just as many churches in which the relentless swirl of religious activity is designed to divert attention from the hypocrisy and spiritual sterility that eats away from within. We simply can't afford to be fooled into concluding all is well based solely on what we see or hear of them. A reputation without a corresponding real-ity is worthless in the eyes of Jesus Christ. His words of warning are forceful and to the point. We would be well-advised to heed them. To be continued . . .

29

The Perks and Pleasures
of Spiritual Triumph

Revelation 3:1

"You have the reputation of being alive, but you are dead."

If the surrounding culture declares that we, the church, are alive but Jesus says we are dead (Rev. 3:1), something's seriously wrong with our standard of success. Our discernment is seriously flawed. Worse still is when *we ourselves* think we're alive but in fact are dead. All too often, the criteria by which we judge success and the criteria employed by God are vastly at odds. What constitutes good, effective, Christ-exalting ministry is one thing to the world, even to the church, and another thing altogether to God.

As we saw in the previous meditation, this was the case in the church at Sardis, where Jesus declared that they had the reputation of being alive but in fact were dead. By "dead" Jesus didn't mean altogether lifeless or utterly hopeless. Later, in verse 4, he indicates that the church in that city still has "a few . . . who have not soiled their garments." And his appeal to the church that it "wake up, and strengthen what remains . . . and repent" indicates that all is not lost. There is one final chance for renewal and life and hope for the future. But the church is in a sorry state: filled with religiosity, hypocrisy, in many respects only nominally Christian.

That a church could be widely known for its activity and influence, all the while dead in the estimation of Christ, is a frightening, sobering reality. Obviously, what impresses men does not necessarily impress God.

Jon Bloom, director of Desiring God ministries, reminded me in an e-mail that "since our hope is in the God who chooses the smallest seed in the garden to produce the largest tree, chooses a shepherd for his greatest king, chooses fishermen for apostles, and chooses to become a carpenter from Nazareth in his incarnation, we should be encouraged by every advance of the gospel, but very careful about what we judge as impressive or fruitful for long-term."

This ought to make one cautious on reading *The Church Report*'s most recent list of "The 50 Most Influential Christians in America." Some of the individuals are certainly deserving of that label and I pray their influence would spread. But in the case of others, perhaps even the majority, one has to ask: influential for doing and saying and accomplishing *what*?

Nowhere is the disparity between human and divine standards of judgment more vividly seen than in Paul's words in 2 Corinthians 2:14–17:

> But thanks be to God, who in Christ always leads us in triumphal procession, and through us spreads the fragrance of the knowledge of him everywhere. For we are the aroma of Christ to God among those who are being saved and among those who are perishing, to one a fragrance from death to death, to the other a fragrance from life to life. Who is sufficient for these things? For we are not, like so many, peddlers of God's word, but as men of sincerity, as commissioned by God, in the sight of God we speak in Christ.

"There it is!" shouts the preacher of prosperity, health, and wealth. "Triumphal procession! God wants us to win, to have it all, to celebrate in a victory parade our triumph over low self-esteem, low wages, shattered dreams, and all forms of suffering!" Well, that's what many on the list are preaching on a regular basis. Evidently they've convinced enough people to subsidize million-dollar salaries, vacation homes, private jets, and whatever else is "essential" to the fulfillment of their ministry.

Perhaps we should look at Paul's words a bit more closely. In all likelihood they refer to the Roman custom in which a victorious general leads his conquered captives in triumphal procession, typically to their execution. There is an obvious paradox in Paul's use of this familiar metaphor. On the one hand, it is God who leads Paul (and by extension, others who likewise preach the gospel as he does) in triumph. Yet, on the other hand, to be led in triumph by someone else implies captivity and suffering and humiliation. Paul Barnett provides this helpful explanation:

> The metaphor is at the same time triumphal and anti-triumphal. It is as God leads his servants as *prisoners of war* in a victory parade that God spreads the knowledge of Christ everywhere through them. Whereas in such victory processions the prisoners would be dejected and embittered, from this captive's lips comes only thanksgiving to God [v. 14a], his captor. Here is restated the power-in-weakness theme (cf. 1:3–11) that pervades the letter. . . . [Thus], to be sure, his ministry is marked by suffering, but so far from that disqualifying him as a minister, God's leading him *in Christ* as a suffering servant thereby legitimates his ministry. *Christ's humiliation in crucifixion is reproduced in the life of his servant.*[6]

Or, in the words of Ben Witherington, Paul "is not saying that he is being led around in triumph, but rather that, like the captives in a triumphal process, he is being treated rudely while in the service of God."[7] Thus Paul asserts that it is precisely in his weakness and suffering as a captive slave of Christ Jesus that God receives all the glory as the One who is triumphantly victorious. Compare this passage with 1 Corinthians 4:9: "For I think that God has exhibited us apostles as last of all, *like men sentenced to death, because we have become a spectacle to the world, to angels, and to men.*" How many so-called apostolic ministries do you hear citing *that* verse today (see also 1 Cor. 4:10–13)?

But there's more. It was also customary for those being led in this procession to disperse incense along the way, perhaps an allusion to the Old Testament sacrifice and the odor of smoke that ascended to heaven, in which God took unique pleasure. Thus Paul portrays his proclamation of the gospel as an unseen yet powerful fragrance permeating the lives of his hearers. "As God drags Paul around as his slave, the knowledge of Christ emanates from [him] wherever he goes."[8]

Observe Paul's imagery: knowing Jesus is like a sweet aroma. There is a spiritual and emotional pleasure in knowing Jesus that can best be compared to the physical delight we experience when our nostrils are filled with the fragrance of the choicest of perfumes or the soothing aroma of our favorite food. Simply put, knowing Jesus smells good!

Those who hear this message are divided into two, and *only* two, groups: those "who are being saved" and "those who are perishing" (see 1 Cor. 1:18). The message of Christ is itself responsible for dividing the hearers in this way. Neutrality is not an option. To the one, Paul's message is a fragrant aroma, a life-sustaining spiritual oxygen; to the other, a repulsive stench, a poisonous gas that suffocates and kills.

Note well: the preacher, whether Paul or you, is a pleasing fragrance to God simply for being faithful to proclaim Christ Jesus. We are a fragrance to God even when our message is rejected. Whether our efforts lead to life or death, we remain an aroma of Christ to God (2 Cor. 2:15a). We have succeeded when we preach Jesus truly and biblically. It is not within our power to convert our hearers. Our success, ultimately, is not measured by the number of our converts, or the proportion of saved to lost, but by the integrity and faithfulness with which we preach the gospel of Christ crucified.

Paul contrasts his philosophy of ministry with those who, according to 2 Corinthians 2:17, are "peddlers of God's word." The word translated "peddling" (*kapeleuo*) is found only here in the New Testament. The related noun form (*kapelos*) was virtually synonymous with the idea of a merchant who regularly cheated his customers by misrepresenting his product in order to increase his profit. Thus the idea is of someone who tampers with the gospel, perhaps eliminating, or at least minimizing, its offensive elements, or altering certain theological points so that the finished product will be more appealing to the audience. Their aim is to gain as great a reputation, as large a following, and as lucrative an offering as possible.

I fear that the triumphalism so prevalent in our pulpits today is a far cry from what Paul had in mind in 2 Corinthians 2. But don't many of these fifty "most influential Christians" have impressive credentials that authenticate the validity of their ministries? Perhaps, but I'm more impressed by the credentials Paul cites in 2 Corinthians 11:23–33 to vindicate his apostolic authority when he was challenged by the false teachers in Corinth. What does the apostle list on his resume? Well, let's see:

Far greater labors, far more imprisonments, with countless beatings, and often near death. Five times I received at the hands of the Jews the forty lashes less one. Three times I was beaten with rods. Once I was stoned. Three times I was shipwrecked; a night and a day I was adrift at sea; on frequent journeys, in danger from rivers, danger from robbers, danger from my own people, danger from Gentiles, danger in the city, danger in the wilderness, danger at sea, danger from false brothers; in toil and hardship, through many a sleepless night, in hunger and thirst, often without food, in cold and exposure. And, apart from other things, there is the daily pressure on me of my anxiety for all the churches. Who is weak, and I am not weak? Who is made to fall, and I am not indignant? If I must boast, I will boast of the things that show my weakness.

Ah, the perks and pleasures of spiritual triumph!

30

Wake Up!

Revelation 3:2–3

"I know your works. You have the reputation of being alive, but you are dead. Wake up, and strengthen what remains and is about to die, for I have not found your works complete in the sight of my God. Remember, then, what you received and heard. Keep it, and repent. If you will not wake up, I will come like a thief, and you will not know at what hour I will come against you."

L et's get right to the point. This letter to the church in Sardis ought to alert us to the fact that a church can be confident of its place in the community, increasing in membership, energetic in its religious activities, liquid in its financial assets, fervent in its outreach to the broader culture, and yet be dead.

I fear it is precisely those reading this who say in response, "Yes, but that's not us," who are particularly in jeopardy. It is the unsuspecting church, the unexamined church, the spiritually smug church that simply can't believe that a congregation that appears to have been so richly blessed by God—"After all, look at how many turned out for our Christmas pageant!"—could possibly be the focus of a divine rebuke such as we find in the words to Sardis.

Take a closer look with me at our Lord's words of warning. The particular problem that moved our Lord to speak in such forceful terms is found in the phrase "I have not found your works complete in the sight of my God" (v. 2b). What is Jesus saying? A brief glance at the list of works in 2:19 will help: love, faith, service, patient endurance. All these were no doubt evident in Sardis, but in a hypocritical, haphazard, halfhearted, or again, incomplete way.

Perhaps their motives were wrong. Perhaps they performed the deeds well enough, but did so for selfish, even mercenary reasons. The words "in the sight of my God" indicate that whereas their deeds may gain human approval, God's evaluation was another matter. George Ladd has a suggestion:

> The church was not troubled by persecution; it was not disturbed by heresy; it was not distressed by Jewish opposition; it was well known as an active, vigorous Christian congregation, characterized by good works and charitable activities. But in the sight of God, all of these religious activities were a failure because they were only formal and external, and not infused with the life-giving Holy Spirit.[9]

Their efforts were perfunctory, lacking that zeal informed by knowledge, noted for beginnings that rarely or ever came to anything of lasting worth. They were the works of a church that had become *addicted to mediocrity*. They were, in a word, wishy-washy.

This is stunning. The world looked at this congregation and said: "Wow! What impressive works you've performed. What a powerful impact you've had. You've done so much for so many." God looked at this congregation and said: "You're dead. I admit, your works are many, but they are motivated by pride and greed, and are driven by a desire that *you* be known as great rather than that *I* be known as great."

Sardis may well be the first church in history to have been filled with what we call today nominal Christians (see Isa. 29:13; Matt. 15:8–9; 23:25–28; 2 Tim. 3:5). Thus far we have noted the marks of the church of which Jesus approves: doctrinal orthodoxy, suffering for Christ's name's sake, love, growth, and now at Sardis we learn of the importance of reality, genuineness, authenticity, and a lifestyle that matches profession.

Our Lord's instruction begins with the exhortation, "Wake up, and strengthen what remains and is about to die." Such words leave room for hope, for they indicate that, although death is near, the possibility for renewal remains. There is an ember, so to speak, which is quickly cooling off but may yet be fanned into flames of life if only the appropriate action is taken. There's a slight possibility that "what remains and is about to die" is a reference to individual members of the church, making this a call to the faithful few to minister to those who are languishing in spiritual lethargy.

The exhortation to wake up suggests that a church can experience spiritual slumber, having fallen asleep and thus having become inattentive to what matters most. "You're in a dream state," says Jesus. "You're living in an unreal world created by your own false criteria of what is pleasing to God. Shake yourself awake and return to reality." Being asleep, the church is oblivious to its perilous condition, unaware of the threat it faces. This is no time to take a nap.

If one sleeps incessantly, one becomes weak—sluggish, with slow reflexes, incapable of resisting temptation or fighting the onslaught of the enemy. Not everything has altogether died. But much is on life support, hanging on in spiritual intensive care. Therefore, strengthen what remains of what is good. Apply yourself to revitalize your commitment to Christ and your pursuit of all things holy.

There are three ways this can be done. First, *remember*. Just as Jesus exhorted the Ephesians (2:5), so he also instructs those in Sardis. Past history should challenge them (us) to present endeavor. Recall the blessings of divine grace and be strengthened by the assurance that what God once did he can certainly do again.

Second, *hold fast* (literally, "keep it"; cf. 2:24b–25). You don't need anything new; simply hold firmly to what you've already received. The phrase used here, "received and heard," probably "refers to the Christian traditions transmitted to the Sardinians when their congregation was founded."[10]

Third, *repent*. Stop sinning. Start obeying. When was the last time you witnessed or participated in a church that repented corporately, confessing its failures without pretense or pride, and committed afresh to the main and plain of Holy Scripture?

The threatened chastisement for failure to do so is vivid (see v. 3b). It's unclear whether this refers to an impending coming of Christ in judgment and discipline against the church in Sardis or a broader reference to the second coming of Christ. In either case, the emphasis is on the unexpected, "like-a-thief" nature of the coming. It would seem, however, that since repentance would forestall the need for Christ's coming, a historical visitation in the first century is in view; not the second coming at the end of history.

Most churches rarely if ever consider the potential for Jesus himself taking disciplinary action against (v. 3) them. We envision ourselves solely as individuals who are accountable to him, but rarely do we think in *corporate* terms. The church is more than a collection of individuals: it is a community, in which spiritual solidarity of vision and mission must be embraced and nurtured. There were a few faithful folk in Sardis who hadn't yielded to the problems that plagued the congregation as a whole. But they will inevitably suffer from whatever disciplinary action the Lord might take against the public witness and financial stability and very existence of the church as a whole.

So, in what ways is the contemporary church, perhaps your church, asleep, on the verge of death, facing the sure disciplinary visitation of Christ himself?

It is enough that I point to the abandonment of the centrality and supremacy of Jesus Christ. Most churches would scoff at the suggestion they are anything less than Christ-centered. But how does our professed commitment to being christocentric express itself in how we worship, in the frequency and fervency with which we celebrate the Eucharist, in what we sing, in how firmly we embrace and how loudly we publicly confess our theological convictions?

How does our alleged christocentricity make itself felt in the way we instruct or merely entertain our children in Sunday school, or the way we evangelize our community, or how consistently we unpack in our preaching the inspired and authoritative word that Christ himself has given us in Scripture?

If we are as energized and driven by the supremacy of Christ as we allege, would visitors to our Sunday service, or to a small group meeting on Thursday night, immediately recognize it? When our annual report is published in January, would the centrality of Jesus Christ be seen in how funds were used, in how missionaries were supported, in the sort of literature we purchase for the church library and bookstore, in the criteria by which elders and deacons are selected to serve?

This letter was then and is now a literal wake-up call for the church(es) of Jesus Christ. If unheeded, we may well experience a visitation from the Lord, but one unlike what we hoped for.

31

An Unstained Remnant

Revelation 3:4–5a

"Yet you have still a few names in Sardis, people who have not soiled their garments, and they will walk with me in white, for they are worthy. The one who conquers will be clothed thus in white garments, and I will never blot his name out of the book of life."

The last few meditations, I admit, have been somewhat negative in that I have portrayed the plight of the church, both in the first century and in our day, in pessimistic terms. I'm not apologizing for that, in view of the fact that we have explicit biblical warrant from the text in Revelation 2–3.

But it would be a mistake to throw in the towel when it comes to the local church or to conclude that it is irredeemable or that its influence is so minimal as to justify the creation of a new model or new expression for being the people of God.

This, it seems, is what George Barna is suggesting in his book *Revolution*. He documents the exodus from the local church of countless folk he calls "Revolutionaries." Finding the local church to be excessively authoritarian, out of touch with the spiritual needs of its members, devoted primarily to its own preservation and comfort, and without much of a witness or influence in the surrounding society, many are simply walking away and allegedly finding satisfaction for their spiritual needs through other expressions of religious life.

I have provided an extensive, three-part review of Barna's book elsewhere,[11] so I won't repeat myself here. I will, however, say this. Nowhere in these seven letters in Revelation 2–3 does Jesus even remotely suggest that the local church is dispensable. Notwithstanding his promised disciplinary visitation to those congregations that refuse to repent, there is no indication he envisioned his people living out their lives together and pursuing the values and goals of the kingdom of God any other way than through the ministry of the local church.

We see this in his letter to the church at Sardis. As bad as it was, and it was *really* bad, there were still a few names in Sardis, people who had not "soiled their garments" who were promised that they will walk with Jesus in white, for they are worthy (v. 4).

In a word, there was in the church at Sardis, as there most likely is in all churches, a faithful, believing, godly remnant that had refused to compromise its convictions, and which the Lord is determined to bless and favor with his manifest presence and goodness.

Our Lord uses an interesting word in verse 4, declaring that these of the remnant have not soiled or stained (Gk. *moluno*) their garments. G. K. Beale believes this term is evidence that the sin of the majority was either idolatry or a decision to suppress their witness by assuming a low profile in idolatrous contexts of the pagan culture in which they had daily interaction. He points out that "soiled" (*moluno*) is used elsewhere in Revelation for the threat of being polluted by the stain of idolatry (see 14:4, 6–9).[12]

I see nothing in this passage or anywhere else in the New Testament that would lead me to believe that the solution to idolatry or immorality or any other pervasive problem is the abandonment of the local church or the decision to seek God via some alternative movement. Yes, sometimes it is necessary to leave a particular local congregation. But this must always be with a view to planting or joining another one. We are not required to remain in a church or denomination that has abandoned the gospel or has seriously compromised its ethical posture or refuses to acknowledge the supreme authority of Scripture, although I think, at times, Christians are too quick to leave; church hopping is not a sanctioned biblical sport! What is clear is that we are *not* free to ignore the New Testament witness concerning the necessity of involvement in a community of

Christians whose corporate life is consistent with the principles of a local church as found, for example, in the pastoral epistles of Paul.

As bad as it was in Sardis, Jesus does not counsel the faithful few to depart. As I noted in the previous meditation, there's a slight possibility that our Lord's exhortation to "strengthen what remains and is about to die" (v. 2) is a reference to individual members of the church, making this a call to the faithful few to minister to those who are languishing in spiritual lethargy. Even if not, Jesus envisions them remaining within the church at Sardis and laboring for its renewal.

The reward promised to those who persevere is fourfold, two of which I'll note briefly here.

First, in verse 4, they "will walk with [Jesus] in white, for they are worthy." Some see a reference here to the resurrection body, but this is more likely a promise of victory and irrevocable purity both in the intermediate state and in the messianic kingdom when those who have remained faithful will experience the consummation of fellowship with Jesus. The reference to white probably refers to the righteousness imputed to us in the act of justification, although we can't dismiss the possibility that Jesus has in mind the experiential purity of life for which he, in verse 4 and elsewhere in these seven letters (cf. Rev. 2:2–3, 9–10, 13, 19; 3:8, 10), commends them.

Second, the overcomer or conqueror will be "clothed . . . in white garments" (v. 5a; cf. 3:18; 6:11; 7:9–14; 19:13). Again, this refers to both the experiential holiness of life now by virtue of the gracious, sanctifying work of the Spirit (cf. Rev. 19:6–8) and the righteousness of Christ himself that is imputed to us by faith.

I'll close with two important comments. First, the language of the saints being clothed in white garments is consistently used in Revelation for those who have persevered through suffering (see especially 6:9–11; 7:9, 13–14). In other words, refusing to accommodate or conform to the behavior of the crowd came at a high price. It's rarely easy to be in the minority, especially when it costs you a job, or a promotion, or popularity, or perhaps even your physical safety and freedom. These "few" in Sardis no doubt suffered intensely for their commitment, but the reward made it all worthwhile.

Second, I also believe Jesus wants us to understand and appreciate the emotional, perhaps even psychological, implications of this truth. What I mean is this: all too often those who know Christ and, by grace, wholeheartedly desire to walk in purity of life fail to fully embrace and enjoy their status as God's forgiven children. They wallow in shame over sins long since confessed and of which they've sincerely repented. Contrary to their status as the adopted and justified children of God, they feel condemned and struggle to walk in the liberty and joy of the elect.

If that is you, remember this: God sees you in his Son! Although your clothing in white will be consummated in the age to come, you are now and forever will be a pure, spotless bride in his sight (cf. 2 Cor. 11:2; Eph. 5:26–27; Rev. 19:7). This glorious truth is not to be perverted into an excuse to sin but is an incentive, by God's grace, to live passionately and resolutely in the pursuit of a practical purity that conforms ever more to the standing we already have in him.

32

The Book of Life
and the Security of the Saints

Revelation 3:5–6

"The one who conquers will be clothed thus in white garments, and I will never blot his name out of the book of life. I will confess his name before my Father and before his angels. He who has an ear, let him hear what the Spirit says to the churches."

The promise to those who conquer continues in Revelation 3:5, a passage that has stirred considerable discussion and controversy. "The one who conquers," said Jesus, "will be clothed thus in white garments, and I will never blot his name out of the book of life. I will confess his name before my Father and before his angels. He who has an ear, let him hear what the Spirit says to the churches."

Some are frightened by this or filled with anxiety that perhaps one day they will fail to conquer and thus have their name blotted out of the book of life. Others read it as a glorious promise of security, a solid rock of assurance, a declaration by Jesus himself that our names will *never* be deleted from God's eternal register. Let's begin our study of it by trying to identify what the "book" is that Jesus mentions. There are at least five possibilities.

1) Colin Hemer refers to one particular custom in ancient Athens according to which the names of condemned criminals were erased from civic registers before their execution. The Greek word translated "to erase" (*exaleiphein*) "was the technical term for such

degradation."[13] As insightful as this may be, it is more likely that we should look for a biblical background to this imagery.

(2) In the Old Testament, the "book of life" (or its equivalents) was a register of the citizens of the theocratic community of Israel. To have one's name written in the book of life implied the privilege of participation in the temporal blessings of the theocracy, while to be erased or blotted out of this book meant exclusion from those blessings. In other words, this book had reference to the rights of citizenship for the Jewish people (cf. Ex. 32:32; Ps. 69:28; Isa. 4:3).

(3) The concept of a book was also used to portray God's all-inclusive decree (Ps. 139:16); i.e., the very days of one's life are ordained and written in God's "book" before one of them occurs.

(4) There is also the notion of books of judgment in which are recorded men's deeds. They serve as that by which or from which one shall be judged (Dan. 7:10; Rev. 20:12).

(5) The most vivid usage, however, is the concept of the book as the register of those who have been chosen for salvation from eternity past. It is not temporal or earthly blessings that are in view, but participation in the eternal kingdom of God as recipients of eternal life (see Luke 10:20; Phil. 4:3; Heb. 12:23; Rev. 13:8; 17:8). It would appear from these texts that not all are written in this book, but only the elect.

If it is this fifth and final view which Jesus had in mind, and I believe it is, there are three possible interpretations.

On the one hand, Jesus may be saying that it is possible for sinning, unrepentant Christians—there were many at Sardis—to fail to overcome or conquer and thereby to forfeit their place in the book of life. Their names, already inscribed in the book, will be erased, signifying the loss of their salvation.

Others suggest that to have one's name blotted out refers to something other than salvation. In Revelation 3:1 Jesus referred to the people at Sardis as having a "name" for being alive, i.e., they had a reputation for spiritual vitality. The idea, then, is that such people are saved, but will forfeit any hope of an honorable position in the coming kingdom of God. They are saved, but will experience shame at the last day. It is not the loss of life, per se, but the loss of a certain quality of life that otherwise could have been theirs. Thus, what one loses by having his or her name erased from the book of life is eternal rewards in the kingdom.

Several factors lead me to conclude that John does *not* envision the possibility of a true Christian forfeiting salvation. We should begin by noting that all of the other promises to the conqueror or overcomer are coined in positive terms with no threat, either implied or explicit, of losing a salvation once gained (see 2:7, 11, 17, 26–27; 3:12, 21). This isn't to suggest that Christians can't backslide and sin badly. The rebukes in these seven letters indicate otherwise. Nevertheless, the evidence of the reality of true saving faith is perseverance, i.e., overcoming (cf. 1 John 2:19).

If it is asked why this promise is couched in negative terms, the answer is obvious: Jesus couldn't say, "I will write his name in the book of life," because the names of the overcomers, i.e., the elect, were *already* written in the book from eternity past (see Rev. 13:8; 17:8). There is no indication in Scripture, least of all in Revelation, of additional names being inscribed in the book as a reward for faithfulness or perseverance. Rather, faithfulness and perseverance are the evidence or fruit of having had one's name written in the book. Those who worship the beast do so precisely because their names were not written in the book in eternity past (13:8; 17:8).

We need to look more closely at Revelation 13:8 and 17:8 to understand what our Lord is saying in 3:5. According to 13:8, ". . . all who dwell on earth will worship it [the beast], everyone whose name has *not been written before the foundation of the world in the book of life of the Lamb who was slain*" (Rev. 13:8). Similarly, in 17:8, "The beast that you saw was, and is not, and is about to rise from the bottomless pit and go to destruction. And the dwellers on earth whose names have not been written in the book of life from the foundation of the world will marvel to see the beast, because it was and is not and is to come."

Note carefully that there are two, and only two, groups of people. On the one hand are those whose names have *not* been written in the book of life from eternity past. They worship and marvel at the beast. The second group consists of those whose names have been written in the book of life, which constitutes the reason why they refuse to give their allegiance to the enemy of Christ. Nowhere does it suggest a third group: people whose names had been written in the book in eternity past but, because they worshiped the beast, failed to overcome or conquer and thus have their names blotted out.

In other words, as John Piper explains, "having our name in the book of life from the foundation of the world seems to mean that God will keep you from falling and grant you to persevere in allegiance to God. Being in the book means you *will* not apostatize."[14] Or again, being written in the book means that God is committed to guarding your heart so that you will conquer and overcome the beast by not yielding to the temptation to worship his name or receive his mark.

Those who worship the beast do so because their names *were not* in the book. Having one's name written in the book from eternity past is what guarantees a life that overcomes, a life that perseveres, a faith that conquers. Piper summarizes:

> This fits with Revelation 3:5, "He who overcomes . . . I will not erase his name from the book of life." The triumph *required* in 3:5 is *guaranteed* in 13:8 and 17:8. This is not a contradiction any more than for Paul to say, "Work out your salvation . . . for God is at work in you to will and to do his good pleasure" (Philippians 2:12–13). It is not nonsense to state the condition: if you conquer, God will not erase your name (3:5); *and* to state the assurance: if your name is written, you will conquer (13:8 and 17:8). God's "written-down-ones" really *must* conquer, and really *will* conquer. One side highlights our responsibility; the other highlights God's sovereignty.[15]

Therefore, this declaration of Jesus is a promise to the elect that nothing will ever, by any means (he uses a double negative), prevent them from possessing the eternal inheritance to which they have been ordained. In other words, we must take note of what Jesus does *not* say. He does not say that anyone will be erased from the book of life. Rather, he says the overcomers will not be erased. His word is a promise of security to overcomers, not a threat of insecurity to those who lapse. So again, Jesus nowhere says he will erase names previously inscribed in the book of life.

When the disciples returned to Jesus, celebrating their victory over the power of the devil, our Lord responded by alerting them to an even greater, more glorious, indescribably reassuring truth: "Nevertheless, do not rejoice in this, that the spirits are subject to you, but rejoice that your names are written in heaven" (Luke 10:20).

What joy! What comfort! What incentive to love him and praise him and serve him. Jesus will *never* blot my name out of the book of life.

33

He Knows My Name

Revelation 3:5–6

"The one who conquers will be clothed thus in white garments, and I will never blot his name out of the book of life. **I will confess his name before my Father and before his angels.** He who has an ear, let him hear what the Spirit says to the churches."

I'm amazed at how seemingly little things in life can have such a massive impact on other people. Take, for example, when someone remembers your name. Perhaps it's a person you admire greatly, whom you've met only once before, but he or she instantly smiles upon seeing your face and says, "Hey, Mike, how are you? It's good to see you again." You feel affirmed and honored that someone who is well known and successful actually knows who you are. Maybe that's because it strokes your ego and awakens personal pride. Whatever the case, no one can deny how good it feels.

Or consider the converse, when you find yourself in the presence of a person who has either forgotten your name or, for whatever reason, has little desire to be seen with you. We've all been in these situations—at least I have!—and they are undeniably painful. You get the distinct impression that you're an embarrassment to that person. When he walks by he pretends to be occupied with other matters, perhaps even turning his back on you. The discomfort is almost tangible. If pressed about who you are, he quickly diverts the focus of the conversation to something less threatening. Ouch!

It's precisely this sort of relational phenomenon that makes the words of Jesus in Revelation 3:5 so powerful and so glorious. Here we find the fourth and final promise to the faithful in Sardis. He's already assured them they will walk with him in white, that they will be clothed in white garments, and that he will never, by no means ever, blot their names out of the book of life. To these Jesus adds: "I will confess his name before my Father and before his angels" (Rev. 3:5b).

Revelation 3:5 actually appears to be a combination of two statements found on the lips of Jesus in the Gospels. In Matthew 10:32 he declared, "So everyone who acknowledges me before men, I also will acknowledge *before my Father* who is in heaven." Again, in Luke 12:8, we read, "And I tell you, everyone who acknowledges me before men, the Son of Man also will acknowledge *before the angels* of God."

Let's unpack this remarkable promise with several observations.

First, this is no grudging concession on the part of Jesus, but a joyful and heartfelt proclamation to the Father and the myriads of angelic beings: "He's mine! She belongs to me! They are worthy!" The words *acknowledge* and *confess* often suggest a reluctant admission on the part of the person speaking, less a willing declaration than a concession to the unavoidable.

That's not what Jesus has in mind when he uses these words. These names are on his lips because they are first in his heart. Jesus isn't embarrassed by those whom he confesses before the Father. He doesn't worry what the angels might think that he would dare speak your name or mine in their presence.

We all know what it's like to feel embarrassed to be in the company of certain people, fearful they might bring reproach on us or cost us standing in the sight of our peers. I'm not suggesting that's a good thing, but whatever the reasons that make us hesitant to be seen with them, it happens. Not Jesus! He is not ashamed (Heb. 2:11) to call us brethren. He rejoices that we are his, and he happily speaks each name with delight and satisfaction.

A second thing to note is that Jesus evidently will speak each of our names individually. Yes, we are the body of Christ, the church, the bride whom he loves with an everlasting love. Our corporate identity as the people of God is an indescribable blessing. But according to Revelation 3:5 Jesus says, "I will confess *his name* [singular]," not merely "their names" before the Father and the angels. People on earth may forget your name or feel uneasy in your presence or reluctantly concede your accomplishments. But Jesus knows your name and will say to the Father, "This is Steve. He is righteous in me. Father, this is Susan. She is mine!"

How does one put in words the thrill and life-giving power of hearing Jesus speak your name? Mary Magdalene has been much in the news of late, especially with the release of Dan Brown's book and then the movie by the same title, *The Da Vinci Code*. Were she present today I hardly think she would care that everyone knew her name, and certainly not for *that* reason. But there was one occasion when it meant more than all the world to her.

Following the resurrection of Jesus, she stood outside the tomb, weeping. Turning around, she "saw Jesus standing, but she did not know that it was Jesus. Jesus said to her, 'Woman, why are you weeping? Whom are you seeking?' Supposing him to be the gardener, she said to him, 'Sir, if you have carried him away, tell me where you have laid him, and I will take him away.' Jesus said to her, 'Mary.' She turned and said to him in Aramaic, 'Rabboni!' (which means Teacher)" (John 20:14b–16).

Do you know the difference between being called "woman" and being called "Mary"? One lady did! This woman, at one time indwelt and tormented by seven demons (Luke 8:2), filled with shame and reproach, hears the sweetest and most comforting word imaginable—her name, "Mary." But it wasn't the name so much as the man on whose lips it was willfully, happily, and confidently found: Jesus! "He knows my name. He remembers me. I'm not an embarrassment to him. He's not ashamed of me!"

This is what each of us who knows him will experience one day, without reservation or qualification. He will speak your name and my name before his Father and the angels.

But this is more than merely hearing your name called as if a teacher is taking roll. This is no perfunctory ritual as Jesus reels off one name after another, to which you respond, "Here," "Yo!" or "Present." This is an open, glad-hearted, public acknowledgment, an owning by Jesus of you and me. "Father, these are the ones you gave me out of all flesh (John 17:2). I declare them to you now.

I proclaim their names as those who have come to faith and have rested in what I've done alone, without looking to another lover, another savior, or another god."

Third, could it be that Jesus speaks our names as he reads them from the book of life? In view of the immediately preceding context (Rev. 3:5a), we can't dismiss the possibility that the names he speaks, one after another, were those that had been written down in that glorious volume from before the foundation of the world (cf. Rev. 13:8; 17:8).

But won't Satan be present to object, to bring up every sin and failure and fault, reminding God and the angels of how often we fell short, repented, only then to fall short again? Well, I'm not sure Satan will be present on that day, but if he is, let your fears be put to rest, for "who shall bring any charge against God's elect? It is God who justifies. Who is to condemn? Christ Jesus is the one who died—more than that, who was raised—who is at the right hand of God, who indeed is interceding for us" (Rom. 8:33–34).

Fourth, there may well be a legal or forensic dimension to this declaration by Jesus of the names of those in the book of life. This isn't at all to diminish the personal and relational reality of what will occur, but only to emphasize that this is our *final vindication* from all charges; it is Christ's declaration that we are righteous through faith in him alone. It is, in a word, our ultimate and eternal "justification."

Fifth, and finally, given the context of both the two references in the Gospels where this statement is found (see above on Matt. 10:32 and Luke 12:8) and the situation envisioned among the churches in Asia Minor, it may be that the emphasis is on confessing the name of the Christian who has bravely confessed the name of Christ in the face of persecution. His confessing our name comes only after we, by the grace of God, have confessed his name to an unbelieving world, willing to endure whatever negative consequences that might bring (cf. Matt. 10:33; Luke 12:9).

Envision the scene. You are standing in the blazing presence of the immeasurable and unfathomable God, an all-consuming fire, the God of infinite and unending glory, the God of unsearchable and incomparable righteousness. Small, frail, weak as you are, Jesus takes hold of your hand and leads you before his Father and beneath the penetrating gaze of myriads of angels. Then he proudly and happily and joyfully and confidently declares: "Father, Sam is mine. I am his. He is clothed in white. I've paid his debt. I suffered his penalty. He is clean. He is pure. He is in me and I in him. Sam is righteous!"

He knows my name. And if you know his, he also knows yours.

Part 6

The Church in Philadelphia

And to the angel of the church in Philadelphia write: "The words of the holy one, the true one, who has the key of David, who opens and no one will shut, who shuts and no one opens. I know your works. Behold, I have set before you an open door, which no one is able to shut. I know that you have but little power, and yet you have kept my word and have not denied my name. Behold, I will make those of the synagogue of Satan who say that they are Jews and are not, but lie—behold, I will make them come and bow down before your feet and they will learn that I have loved you. Because you have kept my word about patient endurance, I will keep you from the hour of trial that is coming on the whole world, to try those who dwell on the earth. I am coming soon. Hold fast what you have, so that no one may seize your crown. The one who conquers, I will make him a pillar in the temple of my God. Never shall he go out of it, and I will write on him the name of my God, and the name of the city of my God, the new Jerusalem, which comes down from my God out of heaven, and my own new name. He who has an ear, let him hear what the Spirit says to the churches."

34

On Behalf of the Mini-church

Revelation 3:7–11

"And to the angel of the church in Philadelphia write: 'The words of the holy one, the true one, who has the key of David, who opens and no one will shut, who shuts and no one opens.'"

One could make a strong case that the letters to Smyrna and Philadelphia are the most important of the seven, for in neither of them do we find a single word of complaint. They both receive unqualified praise and approval. These, then, are truly churches of which Christ heartily approves.

What makes this all the more remarkable is the statement by Jesus in Revelation 3:8 that the church in Philadelphia has "but little power." This isn't a rebuke. It's a commendation. Let me clarify that. Jesus isn't saying that having little power is inherently and always good. He's simply saying that having little power isn't inherently and always bad.

In spite of your lack of size and influence, says Jesus, you faithfully kept my word and, in the face of persecution and perhaps even martyrdom, refused to deny my name. People threatened you. The culture mocked you. The Jewish community slandered you (cf. v. 9). The temptation to jump ship must have been intense. Yet you stood firm. Your lack of resources, money, and manpower proved no obstacle to your accomplishing great things for the kingdom of God!

It's reassuring to know that size is no measure of success. As I've noted before, there is no sin in size, but neither is there in smallness. There are temptations in both circumstances. Those with little power can become bitter and resentful of those who outwardly prosper. Those with great power can become arrogant and condescending toward those of less stature. The mini-church may be tempted to think they've missed the mark or failed to articulate a vision that is pleasing to God. The mega-church may point to their sizeable offerings and overflowing crowds as indicative of divine approval. They could both be wrong.

We don't know if the Christians in Philadelphia were despondent or mired in self-doubt. But the fact that Jesus applauds their efforts in spite of their modest dimensions would suggest they needed this word of encouragement. Our Lord's declaration of what he has and will continue to do on their behalf (see vv. 8–11) is worthy of our close consideration. But first we need to look at his description of himself in verse 7.

Who is this one who speaks such uplifting words to this tiny congregation? He is "the holy one, the true one, who has the key of David, who opens and no one will shut, who shuts and no one opens" (v. 7).

I can't be dogmatic on this point, but I strongly suspect that at the heart of their having "kept his word" and having "refused to deny his name" is their holding forth of Jesus as he has described himself to them. In other words, notwithstanding the vile threats and taunts they endured on a daily basis, these believers proclaimed Jesus as the holy one, the true one, the one who has the key of David.

The Philadelphian believers did more than simply *not* deny the name of Jesus. They loudly and proudly proclaimed him as the Holy One. Their boast was not in their property or multiplicity of programs but in the Holy One of Israel. This title is likely derived either from Isaiah 40:25, where Yahweh asks, "To whom then will you compare me, that I should be like him?" or from Isaiah 43:15 where he again proclaims, "I am the LORD, your Holy One, the Creator of Israel, your King" (see also Job 6:10; Ezek. 39:7; Hos. 11:9; Hab. 1:12; 3:3). According to Isaiah 57:15, his very name is Holy.

There is none with whom he can be compared or against whom he fails to measure up. He is altogether unique, transcendently other, truly in a class by himself. And note well: this glorious, almost indescribable, attribute of God is here predicated of Jesus. As I have written elsewhere,[1] holiness is that in virtue of which God alone is God alone. Holiness is moral majesty.

Does your church have but little power? Do you doubt the legitimacy of your existence? Do you wonder if your sacrifice is worth the effort? Perhaps the kingdom would be better off without you. If the Philadelphians were inclined to think in this way, I suspect they renewed their strength and re-ignited their passion by reflecting on the beauty of divine holiness. "He, our Lord, is the Holy One. How can we not keep his word and proclaim his name, for he is holy, he is ours, and we are his."

Second, he is called "the true one." To the Greek mind this would mean "genuine," or what is real and thus corresponds to reality. To the Hebrew mind it means "faithful" and "trustworthy," deserving of our confidence, dependable, reliable, consistent, and steadfast (see Ex. 34:6; Num. 23:19; Deut. 7:9; Ps. 146:5–6; Lam. 3:22–23; 2 Tim. 2:13). No one ever trusted our God and Savior, the Lord Jesus Christ, in vain!

Third, he is the one "who has the key of David." This is an allusion to Isaiah 22:22 and the role of Eliakim, steward of the household, who was given authority to control who was either admitted to or excluded from the king's presence. This position was quite prominent, perhaps only secondary to the king himself. The point is that Jesus alone has the key to the Davidic or messianic kingdom and that he alone has the undisputed authority to admit or exclude from the New Jerusalem.

Fourth, and finally, he is the one "who opens and no one will shut, who shuts and no one opens." When he opens to his followers the door of the kingdom, no one can shut them out; and when he shuts the door on those who oppose his cause, none can reverse the decision.

Jesus loves the mini-church. He says it explicitly in Revelation 3:9, about which I will say more later. The greatness of a church is not measured by its membership roll or budgetary prowess, but by the size of the Savior, whom it faithfully honors and passionately praises and confidently trusts. The big church is any church that boasts in a big God, attendance and acreage notwithstanding.

Were the Philadelphians envied by any? Probably not. Yet they had no lack, at least in what mattered. Keeping Christ's word and not denying his name is easy for those who know him well. When he is small and unknown, he becomes dispensable, deniable, and easily dismissed for the sake of some grand vision of church growth. A mega-church without a mega-Christ is of little benefit to anyone. A mini-church with a mega-Christ makes them big in the eyes of him whose opinion is the only one that matters.

35

Holy Stubbornness

Revelation 3:8

"Behold, I have set before you an open door, which no one is able to shut."

I've mentioned before that one of my spiritual mentors was often heard to say, "Whatever God requires he provides; whomever God chooses, he changes; and whatever God starts, he finishes." I'd like to add a fourth: "Whatever God promises, he fulfills."

That's incredibly reassuring, especially for those who struggle with doubt and uncertainty and the fear that one day, notwithstanding the promises in his Word, God will pull the rug out. Life has taught us, often painfully, that if something appears to be too good to be true, it probably is. Why should it be any different with God? Will he really deliver on what he has declared? Can I trust him?

I think those questions echo ever more loudly in our heads when times are tough. It's a lot easier to believe God when there's money in the bank and our loved ones are healthy and people like us. Maybe that's one reason Jesus spoke so pointedly to the Christians in Philadelphia. Life was anything but easy for the church in that city. The fact that Jesus applauds their perseverance (v. 10a) and faithfulness in keeping his word (v. 8) and commends them for not denying his name (v. 8), more than suggests that they were faced with a relentless temptation to quit. The opposition they faced from the Jewish community only made things worse (v. 9).

They may well have asked themselves, "Could all this mean that Jesus has abandoned us? Are his promises vain and empty? How can we know he's still on our side?"

Jesus speaks directly to such fears with three powerful promises. It is the first one, in Revelation 3:8a, that has caught my attention. Perhaps it's because at first glance it seems so insignificant. I have to confess that before now I took no notice of it. Not anymore! "Behold," said Jesus, "I have set before you an open door, which no one is able to shut."

What is the open door? Is it great opportunity for missionary activity (cf. 1 Cor. 16:9; 2 Cor. 2:12; Col. 4:3)? That's certainly a possibility. But the preceding verse (3:7) spoke of a messianic kingdom, access to which is under the absolute control of Christ. He is the one who possesses the key and can open and shut at his own will. Here in verse 8 he reminds the Christians at Philadelphia who may have been excommunicated from the local synagogue that he has placed before them an open door into the eternal kingdom, and no one can shut them out.

I'm captivated by this promise of our Lord to the church at Philadelphia, because it's a word of assurance to all Christians who face similar threats or assaults from both human and demonic powers in their effort to derail our journey to the celestial city, the New Jerusalem. It's short but sweet, simple but profound, and gloriously to the point of one of our greatest needs: to be reassured by our great God and Savior, Jesus Christ, that we are forever his and that no amount of hardship in this life can undermine our salvation, that no depth of pain or deprivation can interrupt, disrupt, or counteract his divine determination to bring us safely into our eternal reward.

Think about what this statement says concerning our Lord's determination concerning you and your relationship to him. His mind is made up. His will is resolute and unchangeable. His goal is clear and the means to its accomplishment are undertaken with an immutable and omnipotent commitment. There is a sense, then, in which we might reverently speak of his *holy and righteous stubbornness* when it comes to the welfare of his people. He simply won't allow anyone to slam shut the door that he has opened.

The very existence of this open door is ultimately by virtue of his will, not ours. It reminds me of what Jesus said in Matthew: "All things have been handed over to me by my Father, and no one knows the Son except the Father, and no one knows the Father except the Son and anyone to whom the Son chooses to reveal him" (11:27). Or, to use the words of Revelation 3:8, no one knows the Father or will enjoy him forever except those on whose behalf the Son has graciously opened the door to eternal life!

Not all the persecution in the world can reverse his decree. Not all the hatred and animosity of the enemy can tempt him to change his mind. Not all the posturing and strutting of a secular and unbelieving culture can induce him to close the door on those to whom he has decided to open it. Not all the threats, slander, resistance, or any other attempt on the part of the people around us to undermine our relationship with Christ will succeed.

No one is able to shut this door into eternal relationship and intimacy with Jesus, this entrance into eternal joy and life in his presence. No one. Not your worst enemy. Not even those who mock you for your faith. Not Islamic terrorists or economic collapse or a terminal illness. Nothing. Not the collective power of an entire world, not the combined energy of all demonic beings, neither Satan nor any other created being can overturn the decree of Christ who says: These are my people and shall remain so forever.

Often we fear that Satan has the power or freedom to counteract Christ's saving work, or that he can orchestrate a scenario that will lead to our ultimate demise. Or perhaps he can put a stumbling block in our path that will ensnare or entangle us in such a way that not even God himself can extricate us or deliver us from his nefarious strategy. Ah, but who is this God? Is he not the one "who is able to keep you from stumbling and to present you blameless before the presence of his glory with great joy" (Jude 24)?

I'm also reminded of what Paul said in Romans 8:31, a precious passage indeed: "If God is for us, who can be against us?" His purpose isn't to deny that we have enemies. Far from it. Our enemies are numerous and powerful and relentless in their assault against the saints.

His point, rather, is that they will always fail. Yes, they will continue to attack and accuse and adopt an adversarial posture. They can inflict injury, bring disappointment, shatter dreams, and disrupt relationships. But they can never close the door that Christ has opened. Or to use the language of Paul again from Romans 8, they shall never "separate us from the love of Christ" (8:35). Their weapons may include tribulation, distress, persecution, famine, nakedness, danger, and sword (8:35). They may even kill us, treating us "as sheep to be slaughtered" (8:36). But in all these things, yes, in all these horrific experiences, "we are more than conquerors through him who loved us" (8:37), through him who opened the door and allows no one to shut it.

This glorious truth of God's sovereignty in our salvation, far from precluding the need for personal holiness, empowers and undergirds it. We must persevere in our commitment to him, and we shall persevere because of his commitment to us.

There is in the heart of our Lord, as I said, a holy stubbornness. He will not be deterred. His purpose will come to pass. His promise will be fulfilled. No one can close the door he has opened. Entrance into the bliss of eternal joy is assured to those who know Jesus. Praise be to God!

36

Vindication as the Beloved
of God

Revelation 3:9

"Behold, I will make those of the synagogue of Satan who say that they are Jews and are not, but lie—behold, I will make them come and bow down before your feet and they will learn that I have loved you."

Whatever God promises, God fulfills. This marvelous truth puts legs beneath our Lord's declaration that the door he has opened for us no one can shut (v. 8). But there's yet more in his promise to the faithful in Philadelphia and therefore more in his promise to you and me: "Behold, I will make those of the synagogue of Satan who say that they are Jews and are not, but lie—behold, I will make them come and bow down before your feet and *they will learn that I have loved you*" (Rev. 3:9).

We've already encountered the presence of those who lie about being Jewish, so I refer you to my comments there (see Rev. 2:8–9 and Meditation 10). What is especially noteworthy here is how our Lord describes his vindication of those who've remained faithful in the face of persecution. Literally, Jesus says he will give these false Jews of the synagogue of Satan to the church at Philadelphia, i.e., he will cause them to bow down at their feet and to know that Jesus has loved them.

Does this imply that these Jewish opponents will become Christians? Some say yes and contend that the "open door" of verse 8 pertains specifically to evangelistic opportunity and success among the Jewish population of the city. Appeal is also made to the word translated "bow down" (*proskuneo*), used elsewhere on several occasions in Revelation of voluntary worship. However, if they were to be saved, it would be strange for them to bow down *in worship* at the feet of fellow Christians. David Aune is probably right in saying that "this prostration has no religious significance but is simply the traditional (oriental) expression of homage and honor."[2]

It may be that recognition on their part that Jesus loves the church is the occasion, indeed, the stimulus, for their conversion, much in line with Paul's thought in Romans 11 where he describes the Jews being provoked to jealousy upon seeing Gentiles savingly grafted into the olive tree. It must be admitted, however, that "make them to come" is odd language for conversion. Furthermore, the point of their being made to prostrate themselves before Christians is so that they might acknowledge the love Jesus has for the church. But if they are no less converted, i.e., no less Christian, than the church, they too would be the objects of Jesus' saving love. But is it not his point to demonstrate to the persecutors of the church that God's love is precisely for those seemingly insignificant and weak believers in Philadelphia, irrespective of ethnic identity?

Perhaps, then, John has in mind *either* (1) some event or process by which these Jews are compelled to acknowledge that the Philadelphian believers are the beloved people of God and that such status is not the result of ethnic heritage or national affiliation but rather faith in Jesus, *or* (2) the final judgment day at which "every knee shall bow and every tongue confess that Jesus is Lord" (Phil. 2:10–11).

The most intriguing feature of this passage is that it appears to be an allusion to several Old Testament texts in which it is prophesied that Gentiles will come and bow down before Israel in the last days. For example, "The sons of those who afflicted you shall come bending low to you, and all who despised you shall bow down at your feet; they shall call you the City of the LORD, the Zion of the Holy One of Israel" (Isa. 60:14).

In Isaiah 45:14 we read how Gentile peoples will "come over to you [Israel] and be yours; they shall follow you; they shall come over in chains and bow down to you." Once again, "with their faces to the ground they [the Gentiles] shall bow down to you [Israel], and lick the dust of your feet. Then you will know that I am the LORD; those who wait for me shall not be put to shame" (Isa. 49:23).

The irony here is so thick you could cut it with a knife. In all these Old Testament texts it is the Gentiles who grovel before Israel, whereas in Revelation 3:9 it is the Jews who will bow at the feet of this predominantly Gentile Christian church.

The irony intensifies when we note that in Isaiah 60:14 it is the Gentiles who will call the Israelites "the City of the LORD, the Zion of the Holy One of Israel." But now, in Revelation 3:12, the tables are turned: it is the church that is described in such glorious terms. Here we read that the overcomers before whom these Jews prostrate themselves are given the name of "the city of my God, the new Jerusalem." Let us note that the name by which Jesus identifies himself to the Philadelphian believers is "the Holy One" (Rev. 3:7), thereby reinforcing the link between Revelation 3 and Isaiah 60.

We should also note that the words "they will learn that I have loved you" (Rev. 3:7) may be an allusion to Isaiah 43:4: "Because you [Israel] are precious in my eyes, and honored, and I love you." Again this reinforces the notion that Jesus saw in the church the fulfillment of these Old Testament prophetic promises. In other words, the fulfillment of these Isaianic prophecies "will be the reverse of what the Philadelphian Jews expect: *they* will have to 'bow down before *your* feet,' and acknowledge 'that I have loved *you.*' Let the Christians take heart, for it is on them that the Lord has set his favour."[3]

Beyond the theological and eschatological implications of what this says about the church as the true Israel of God is the profoundly encouraging boost it gives to the oppressed heart seeking to stand firm in faith for Jesus. These believers in Philadelphia were no doubt hearing the taunts of their oppressors, similar to what David often lamented in the Psalms: "O LORD, how many are my foes! Many are rising against me; many are saying of my soul, there is no salvation for him in God" (Ps. 3:1–2). Or again, in Psalm 71:11, the psalmist refers to his enemies as declaring, "God has forsaken him; pursue and seize him, for there is none to deliver him."

The pagan world looked with disdain on the church in Philadelphia and concluded that people who suffered in this way must be unloved by their God, if not entirely abandoned by him. Perhaps you've heard similar words: "What kind of God is it who permits his children to endure such pain and oppression? He obviously doesn't love you very much. You matter little to him. Otherwise he'd heal you. If his love were genuine, he'd spare you such distress. Where is he when you need him most? If he cared, he would long ago have delivered you from people like us."

There's no guarantee that vindication will come in this life. We may die with such blasphemous words echoing in our ears. But the affection of our great God will not forever remain hidden from view. Jesus assures us that a day is coming when the world will know, all too painfully, that we are loved with an immutable and infinitely intense passion. All ridicule will be redressed, every scoff will be silenced, each sneer wiped from their faces. Then there will be an indescribable display of divine delight and loud celebration as Jesus will say (shout? sing?), for all to hear, and show, for all to see, that he truly loves his own.

37

Kept from the Hour of Trial

Revelation 3:10–11

"Because you have kept my word about patient endurance, I will
keep you from the hour of trial that is coming on the whole world,
to try those who dwell on the earth. I am coming soon. Hold fast
what you have, so that no one may seize your crown."

I f you've ever wondered whether it matters much to Jesus that
you've kept the faith and maintained your commitment to him,
this promise to the church of Philadelphia should put your fears
to rest.

Sadly, today more attention is given to sensational claims of supernatural exploits than to the routine faithfulness of the average
Christian. Simple virtues like integrity, endurance in the face of pain
and disappointment, persistence in one's struggle with sin, and love
for the brethren aren't the sort that get written up on the *Drudge
Report* or fill the editorial page of *The New York Times*.

But I can assure you that they are of paramount importance to
our Lord. Such resolute commitment to stay the course, spiritually
speaking, may not get your name in the church bulletin or result in
an invitation to appear on the *700 Club*, but it matters preeminently
to Jesus! The world may mock you for it, laugh, and consider you a
fool to sacrifice so much of a monetary and personal nature simply
for the sake of retaining your public and private commitment to
Jesus, but this is no small matter.

If you doubt what I'm saying, look closely at our Lord's words in Revelation 3:10–11: "Because you have kept my word about patient endurance," said Jesus to the church in Philadelphia, "I will keep you from the hour of trial that is coming on the whole world, to try those who dwell on the earth. I am coming soon. Hold fast what you have, so that no one may seize your crown."

Patient endurance is no small feat, especially given our proclivity for impatience, self-preservation, and our desire for personal peace and comfort. Add to this the longing to be liked and the love of money, and you can begin to grasp the significance of our Lord's promise to the faithful.

Now that I've made what I believe is the most important point in this passage, let me turn to the theological controversies that swirl around it.

As you probably know, people often appeal to this text in support of the doctrine of the pre-tribulation rapture of the church. Personally, I don't believe Jesus, or John, had any such thing in mind. A few observations should make this clear.

First, the notion that any Christian is assured of special protection from trials, tribulations, and persecution is unbiblical. We've seen repeatedly in these seven letters that suffering for the sake of Christ and the gospel is something all believers must embrace (see Rev. 2:2–3, 9–10, 13; 3:8–10). According to Paul, it is "through many tribulations [*thlipsis*; the same word used in Rev. 1:9; 7:14] we must enter the kingdom of God" (Acts 14:22). Jesus declared that "in the world you will have tribulation [*thlipsis*]" (John 16:33). Again, we are to "rejoice in our sufferings [*thlipsis*]" (Rom. 5:3; see also John 15:19–20; Acts 5:40-41; 1 Cor. 4:11–13; 2 Cor. 4:7–12; 11:24–25; 2 Tim. 3:12).

Second, the trial or tribulation that is coming is designed for the judgment of *unbelievers*, not Christians. "Those who dwell on the earth" (v. 9) or "earth-dwellers" is a stock phrase in Revelation that always refers to pagan persecutors of the church (6:10; 8:13; 11:10; 12:12; 13:8, 12, 14; 14:6; 17:2, 8). They are the ones who suffer the seal, trumpet, and bowl judgments of Revelation that characterize the entire church age from the first coming of Christ to his second.

Third, the promise, then, is for spiritual protection in the midst of physical tribulation. Jesus is assuring his people that he will provide sufficient sustenance to preserve them in their faith, no matter what they face. The promise here is similar to what we find in Revelation 7:1–3, 13–14 where the people of God are "sealed" lest they suffer spiritual harm from "the great tribulation [*thlipsis*]" (v. 14; cf. Rev. 11:1–2; 12:6, 14–17). Clearly, believers endure and emerge from tribulation spiritually secure. As Beale notes, "They are not preserved from trial by removal from it, but their faith is preserved through trial because they have been sealed by God."[4]

Fourth, pre-tribulationists have typically insisted that the only way God's people can be spiritually protected from the outpouring of divine wrath is by being physically removed from the earth. But this is clearly not the case, as John 17:15 makes clear, as also does the presence of the Israelites in Egypt during the time of the ten plagues. In this passage in John we find the only other place in the New Testament where the precise phrase "kept from" (*tereo ek*) is used. There Jesus prays to the Father, "I do not ask that you take them out of the world, but that you *keep them from* the evil one."

It's important to note in this text that "keep from" is actually contrasted with the notion of physical removal. Jesus prays not that the Father will "take them out of the world" (i.e., physically remove them), but that the Father will "keep them from" Satan's effort to destroy their spiritual life. Thus, when we turn to Revelation 3:10 we see that it is from the wrath of God poured out on "earth-dwellers" (unbelievers) that he promises to keep them. In the face of certain opposition and oppression from Satan, the beast, and unbelievers, this is a glorious promise indeed.

Fifth, we must never forget that it is precisely in remaining faithful unto death that our greatest victory is achieved, not in being "raptured" to safety (cf. Rev. 2:10). Believers conquer Satan and the beast "by the blood of the Lamb and by the word of their testimony, for they loved not their lives even unto death" (Rev. 12:11).

But what, precisely, is "the hour of trial that is coming on the whole world," and when will it occur?

Of one thing I'm certain: the promise of protection must have been of practical benefit and reassurance for the people of the church in Philadelphia in the first century. Thus, contrary to what is argued by Dispensationalists, this "hour of trial" can't be restricted to, although it may be inclusive of, a time of tribulation at the end of the present age.

If you are inclined to insist on a strictly futurist interpretation of the "hour of trial," ask yourself whether it seems odd—dare I say, impossible—that Jesus would promise one church in Asia Minor in the first century that they were to be protected from an event that not one single individual in that church would ever see, indeed, an event that allegedly would not transpire for at least another nineteen-hundred years! How could this "hour of trial" be an event centuries after the Philadelphian Christians lived, especially since their protection from it is the very specific reward to them of their very specific, and historically identifiable, resistance to persecution and steadfast faithfulness in proclaiming the word of God? They are promised protection because they kept the word of Christ's perseverance.

I'm persuaded that Jesus is referring to that tribulation (*thlipsis*) that has already begun for Christians, including the Philadelphians, and will continue throughout the present age. In writing to the churches, John identifies himself as their "brother and partner in the tribulation [*thlipsis*] and the kingdom and the patient endurance that are in Jesus" (Rev. 1:9). In other words, "the hour of trial" is likely a reference to the entire, inter-advent church age, during which there will always be suffering and tribulation for those who stand firm in their witness for Christ.

This isn't to deny that there will emerge an especially intensified and horrific period of tribulation in connection with the return of Christ at the end of history, regardless of how long you conceive it to be. But Jesus must have in mind an experience that was impending or already present for the Philadelphian believers in the first century and for all believers in subsequent centuries of the church's existence.

Jesus concludes with both a word of assurance and an exhortation: "I am coming soon. Hold fast what you have, so that no one may seize your crown" (Rev. 3:11). Is this coming the second advent at the close of history or a first-century disciplinary visitation? Possibly the former, but assuredly not the latter. After all, given the obedience of the Philadelphian church, there was no need for a coming of Jesus to judge or chastise, as was the case with Ephesus in 2:5, Pergamum in 2:16, and Sardis in 3:3.

However, there may be another option. Beale suggests that "the 'coming' referred to in this verse is the increased presence of Christ that will protect these believers when they pass through tribulation, as has just been mentioned in v. 10."[5] In other words, this may be a spiritual coming to provide comfort and the power to persevere, a drawing near to their hearts to energize them in their commitment. His coming or approach to them is not spatial, but spiritual and sanctifying, in which he intensifies his sustaining influence in their souls. If he can "come" to the churches at Ephesus, Pergamum, and Sardis to discipline, he can certainly "come" to the church at Philadelphia to strengthen and bless.

"Hold fast" is the exhortation, lest the reward for faithful and fruitful obedience be taken from them. Those who have until now held fast and patiently endured must continue to persevere. Here again we see the beautiful and altogether harmonious interplay between divine sovereignty and human responsibility. As I said in a previous meditation, we must persevere in our commitment to him, and we shall persevere because of his commitment to us. Even so, come Lord Jesus and preserve us "through faith for a salvation ready to be revealed in the last time" (1 Pet. 1:5).

38

Pillars of Beauty

Revelation 3:12–13

"The one who conquers, **I will make him a pillar in the temple of my God. Never shall he go out of it, and I will write on him the name of my God, and the name of the city of my God, the new Jerusalem, which comes down from my God out of heaven, and my own new name. He who has an ear, let him hear what the Spirit says to the churches.**"

The Bible has a remarkable capacity to challenge and overcome our misperceptions about who we are. When we are inclined to think of ourselves as orphans, the biblical text declares that we are the adopted children of God. If we are wracked with guilt, the inspired Word reminds us that we are forgiven. The feeling of being stained and soiled by sin is overcome with the realization that we are cleansed by the blood of Christ and clothed in his righteousness.

It's much the same when it comes to our place and role in the church. Many are inclined to view themselves as a blight or blemish on the body of Christ, a useless, transient appendage that contributes little to the advance of God's kingdom. Utility becomes the measure of their worth. If they do little, they are little. Feeling ungifted and unqualified, they linger in the shadows, sitting on the back row, rarely if ever asked for their opinion and even less often willing to step forward and contribute positively to the welfare of the body as a whole.

Here in Revelation 3:12–13, the Word of God again graciously reminds us of God's perspective and reverses the paralyzing impact of false perceptions. Our Lord's words of promise and reassurance to those who persevere in faith have bolstered and buoyed our faith throughout the course of these seven letters. Nowhere is this more vividly seen and felt than in his comments to the church at Philadelphia. To the one who conquers, he promises,

> "I will make him a pillar in the temple of my God. Never shall he go out of it, and I will write on him the name of my God, and the name of the city of my God, the new Jerusalem, which comes down from my God out of heaven, and my own new name. He who has an ear, let him hear what the Spirit says to the churches" (Rev. 3:12–13).

Imagery of the individual Christian and the corporate church as the temple of God are familiar ones in Scripture. For example,

> Do you not know that you are God's temple and that God's Spirit dwells in you? If anyone destroys God's temple, God will destroy him. For God's temple is holy, and *you* are that temple. (1 Cor. 3:16–17)

> Or do you not know that your body is a temple of the Holy Spirit within you, whom you have from God? (1 Cor. 6:19)

> . . . in whom the whole structure, being joined together, grows into a holy temple in the Lord. In him you also are being built together into a dwelling place for God by the Spirit. (Eph. 2:21–22)

> As you come to him, a living stone rejected by men but in the sight of God chosen and precious, you yourselves like living stones are being built up as a spiritual house, to be a holy priesthood, to offer spiritual sacrifices acceptable to God through Jesus Christ. (1 Pet. 2:4–5)

The metaphor is obviously fluid and thus there is no inconsistency in affirming that we are both the temple and the pillars within it. In declaring that he will make us pillars, our Lord is honing in on one or perhaps several crucial truths about our relationship with him and our place in his purposes.

There are several Old Testament references that might serve as the possible backdrop for this portrait. We read in 1 Kings 7:13–22 of the two pillars constructed for Solomon's temple, ornate and awesome in their beauty and strength.

The reference to the "pillar" may continue (from Rev. 3:7) the allusion to Isaiah 22:22 where Eliakim's relatives achieve glory by hanging on him as a peg firmly attached to a wall (v. 24). Beale points out that "some Greek OT witnesses even refer to Eliakim as being set up as a 'pillar' in Isa. 22:23."[6] Thus, "in contrast to Eliakim's dependents, who eventually lost their glory and position in the palace when he was finally removed (cf. Isa. 22:23–25), the followers of Jesus will never be removed from their position in the temple/palace because Jesus, the 'true' Messiah, will never lose his regal position in the presence of his Father."[7]

The concept of God's people as a "pillar" is also found in Jeremiah 1:18 where the emphasis is on strength and stability and resistance to attack from the enemy. There is certainly New Testament precedence for describing God's people as "pillars," as seen in 1 Timothy 3:15 and Galatians 2:9.

So what point is Jesus making in Revelation 3:12? In what sense will he make the overcomer a "pillar in the temple" of his God?

A few have suggested that this is an allusion to the custom in which the provincial priest of the imperial cult, at the close of his tenure in office, erected in the temple area his statue or pillar inscribed with his name, together with the name of his father, his home town, and his years in office. However, several have pointed out that little evidence exists for this practice and that Philadelphia didn't even have a temple dedicated to the imperial cult until early in the third century A.D.

Perhaps the language is simply a metaphor of eternal salvation. Special emphasis may be on the security of our position as God's dwelling place in view of the assurance that "never shall he go out of it." This declaration would have carried special significance for those in Philadelphia: although they are expelled from Satan's synagogue (Rev. 3:9), they find a permanent place in God's temple.

Furthermore, as Mounce has noted, "to a city that had experienced devastating earthquakes [a massive quake devastated the city in A.D. 17] which caused people to flee into the countryside and establish temporary dwellings there, the promise of permanence within the New Jerusalem would have a special meaning."[8] Thus, to a people familiar with uncertainty and weakness (cf. 3:8), it certainly conveys the idea of stability and permanence in the believer's relationship with God. H. B. Swete concurs: "As the pillar cannot be moved out of its place while the house stands, so a lapse from goodness will be impossible for the character which has been fixed by the final victory. A *luchnia* [lampstand] may be removed (ii.6), but not a *stulos* [pillar]."[9]

A friend, who wishes to remain anonymous, recently reminded me that the key to this passage may be found in Psalm 144:12: "May our sons in their youth be like plants full grown, our daughters like corner pillars cut for the structure of a palace" or "fashioned as for a palace" (NASB). From this we see that the purpose of a pillar was more than simply to uphold a palace, more than simply to provide support or serve a load-bearing function. Rather, pillars were designed to adorn a palace. Perhaps, then, it is the beauty of a pillar that is in view and not simply its utility.

My friend wrote to me of his many journeys throughout the Middle East and especially of his visits to countless mosques. A number of pillars he saw were made of elaborately hand-carved wood, while others were covered with thousands of individually handcrafted ceramic tiles. He noted that "even the adjective 'opulent' seems too restrained for many of these pillars." More important still, "the degree and level of the craftsmanship of a mosque is always in direct correlation to the status of the builder, its beauty a visible demonstration of the builder's benevolence to the community."

While such pillars may serve practical functions, "their aesthetic beauty deliberately overshadows their usefulness, and for the thoughtful soul this opens a wonderful window into the imagery" of Revelation 3.

"In much of the church world," he astutely notes, "our usefulness is what seems to matter: if we can teach Sunday school, lead an outreach, or organize a committee, then we are 'an asset to the church.' But in his words to the church of Philadelphia, Jesus assures us that our place in God's presence is not based on our utility—he certainly does not need us to uphold his temple!" Rather, we are placed near the King of kings and adorned with his profound spiritual beauty in order to reflect the majesty and graciousness of the

One in whom we "are being built together into a dwelling place for God by the Spirit" (Eph. 2:22).

Whatever struggle may be yours in trying to identify yourself and your place in the kingdom of God, never forget that you are his dwelling place, the heart of his abode, and as a pillar in this temple you will reflect his beauty and splendor forever and ever, never to go out of it, ever.

39

A New Name
for a New Identity

Revelation 3:12–13

"The one who conquers, I will make him a pillar in the temple of
my God. Never shall he go out of it, and I will write on him the
name of my God, and the name of the city of my God, the new
Jerusalem, which comes down from my God out of heaven, and
my own new name. He who has an ear, let him hear what the
Spirit says to the churches."

As mentioned in the previous meditation, Christians often
struggle with a sense of identity. They fail to grasp who
they are by virtue not merely of creation but especially of
regeneration and redemption. A failure to embrace our new identity
and the privileges and responsibilities that come with it can be devastating. Virtually every assault and accusation of Satan is grounded
in his effort to convince us we are not who God, in fact, declares we
are. If the enemy can persuade us that we are spiritual impostors,
interlopers, unwanted and unqualified intruders into the kingdom
of God, his victory is virtually assured.

On the other hand, if I'm able to rest securely in who I am in
Christ, an identity forged by forgiveness, not failure, by his goodness
rather than mine, I am enveloped and enclosed in a veritable fortress
of strength and protective love. No assault will prevail. No accusation will stand. No insinuation, however subtle, will undermine my

confidence or sow seeds of suspicion in my soul. I am who he says I am by virtue of what he has done and will do. It's just that simple.

This is the great practical payoff of a glorious principle based on a God-ordained promise in Revelation 3:12. Look at it again:

> "I will make him a pillar in the temple of my God. Never shall he go out of it, and I will write on him the name of my God, and the name of the city of my God, the new Jerusalem, which comes down from my God out of heaven, and my own new name. He who has an ear, let him hear what the Spirit says to the churches." (Rev. 3:12–13)

If ever you and I needed to "hear what the Spirit says to the churches," it is now. So may God enable us to listen carefully and confidently.

Here is your current identity and ultimate destiny if you know Christ truly. It consists in having inscribed on your body, soul, and spirit the name of God, his city, and his Son. There is, of course, as is the case with virtually all spiritual realities, a sense in which this is already true of us though not yet consummated. What we are now, we shall be in eternal verity, forever.

First, written on us is "the name of my God," says Jesus. There is a rich background in the Old Testament for this statement. One hardly knows where to begin. But let's start with Exodus 28:36–38, where we read:

> "You shall make a plate of pure gold and engrave on it, like the engraving of a signet, 'Holy to the LORD.' And you shall fasten it on the turban by a cord of blue. It shall be on the front of the turban. It shall be on Aaron's forehead, and Aaron shall bear any guilt from the holy things that the people of Israel consecrate as their holy gifts. It shall regularly be on his forehead, that they may be accepted before the LORD." (Ex. 28:36–38)

It doesn't stop there. Consider these several instances of God's people receiving his name:

> "... everyone who is called by my name, whom I created for my glory, whom I formed and made." (Isa. 43:7)

> "I will give in my house and within my walls a monument and a name better than sons and daughters; I will give them an everlasting name that shall not be cut off." (Isa. 56:5)

The nations shall see your righteousness, and all the kings your glory, and you shall be called by a new name that the mouth of the LORD will give. (Isa. 62:2)

"You shall leave your name to my chosen for a curse, and the Lord GOD will put you to death, but *his servants* he will call by another name." (Isa. 65:15)

In the priestly blessing that we often cite today as a benediction, God declares that "so shall they put my name upon the people of Israel, and I will bless them" (Num. 6:27; see also Deut. 28:10 and Dan. 9:18–19).

In ancient times, especially in the world of magic, to know someone's name was to gain power over them. As a counterpoint, then, to be called by God's name certainly suggests his sovereign rights over us as his children. It also points to ownership and consecration: our lives should be dominated and determined by our identity as his own, shaped and fashioned in godliness according to his glorious image.

Second, Jesus promises to inscribe on us "the name of the city of my God, the new Jerusalem, which comes down from my God out of heaven." This should come as no surprise, given what the New Testament says about our citizenship in the New Jerusalem (see Gal. 4:26; Heb. 12:22; Phil. 3:20).

Furthermore, in Revelation 21:2–8 the people of God are virtually identified with the New Jerusalem. In other words, to bear the name of the city of God is more than simply a way of identifying its citizens, its rightful inhabitants. There is also a sense in which we *are* the New Jerusalem (cf. Isa. 56:5; Ezek. 48:35). At minimum it is a way of stressing our permanent and ever-so-intimate presence with God and his presence in and for us, forever.

Lastly, and perhaps most important and precious of all, we shall bear Christ's "own new name." Note the emphatic position of the adjective, literally, "my name, the new." Christ's new name can hardly be any of those with which we are already familiar, such as Lord, Messiah, Savior, Son of God, Son of Man, and Word. "New" (*kainos*) means more than simply different or recent, as over against what one formerly was designated. Here it means *new in quality, belonging to and characterized by the life and values of the new creation* for which we have already been reborn (2 Cor. 5:17).

This "new name" is another way of alerting us to the fact that there awaits us a fuller, indeed infinitely expansive, revelation of the glory and beauty of Christ beyond anything we have seen, heard, or understood in this life. Whatever we know of Christ, however rich the treasures we enjoy of him in the present, whatever knowledge or insight into the unsearchable depths of his wisdom, knowledge, ways, and judgments we are graciously enabled to experience, all is but a sub-microscopic drop in the vast ocean of a spiritually macroscopic revelation yet to come.

Let's also not forget that being given a new name in biblical tradition is most often associated with the idea of receiving a new status, function, or change in character and calling (see Gen. 32:28). I can't even begin to speculate on what this entails for us in the ages to come.

And what, precisely, is this new name? We don't have a clue! In fact, its secrecy or hiddenness is one of its priceless qualities, for an unknown name suggests again that we who are called by it and have it inscribed on our souls are invulnerable to the enemy's attack. What Satan does not know, he cannot destroy. To be called by this new name is to be preserved for fellowship and intimacy with our Lord that none can touch or disrupt.

Part 7

The Church in Laodicea

And to the angel of the church in Laodicea write: "The words of the Amen, the faithful and true witness, the beginning of God's creation. I know your works: you are neither cold nor hot. Would that you were either cold or hot! So, because you are lukewarm, and neither hot nor cold, I will spit you out of my mouth. For you say, I am rich, I have prospered, and I need nothing, not realizing that you are wretched, pitiable, poor, blind, and naked. I counsel you to buy from me gold refined by fire, so that you may be rich, and white garments so that you may clothe yourself and the shame of your nakedness may not be seen, and salve to anoint your eyes, so that you may see. Those whom I love, I reprove and discipline, so be zealous and repent. Behold, I stand at the door and knock. If anyone hears my voice and opens the door, I will come in to him and eat with him, and he with me. The one who conquers, I will grant him to sit with me on my throne, as I also conquered and sat down with my Father on his throne. He who has an ear, let him hear what the Spirit says to the churches."

40

The Most (In)Famous Church of All

Revelation 3:14

"And to the angel of the church in Laodicea write: 'The words of the Amen, the faithful and true witness, the beginning of God's creation.'"

I've lived in eight cities, and I am profoundly grateful for the experiences of each. I was born in Shawnee, Oklahoma, from which we moved when I was ten years old to settle in Midland, Texas. I attended high school in Duncan, Oklahoma, and went to college in Norman. My wife and I lived in Dallas, Texas, for twelve years and then moved back to Oklahoma, this time to Ardmore, in 1985. Since then we've lived in Kansas City, Chicago, and now again in Kansas City.

As I said, I'm grateful for what I experienced in each city. Three of them are relatively small (Shawnee, Duncan, and Ardmore), two are what we might call mid-sized (Midland and Norman), while the other three are among the largest cities in our nation (Dallas, Chicago, and Kansas City). I have no hesitation in claiming them all.

I'm not sure the same could be said for our seventh and final city in Revelation 2–3. Whether or not the citizens of ancient Laodicea were proud of their home town or ashamed of its failures is impossible to know. But of one thing we may be sure; it had massive spiritual problems and called forth the most stringent and stinging rebuke yet issued by our Lord. Indeed, this city, this church, and this letter are the most famous (infamous?) of the seven. A brief introduction to Laodicea, therefore, will prove beneficial in our study of the letter addressed to it.

The courier who had been entrusted by the apostle John with the seven letters to the seven churches neared his journey's end. Having embarked from the island of Patmos with the book of Revelation securely tucked away in his messenger's pouch, he would have begun his travel along the circular route by first visiting Ephesus. Moving northward he would pass through the cities of Smyrna and Pergamum, at which point, turning southeast, his journey would lead him to Thyatira, Sardis, and Philadelphia. Finally, having come almost full circle along the well-beaten trade route, he would arrive at his final destination, Laodicea.

As the courier no doubt tarried in each of the cities long enough to hear the public reading of the respective letters, his understanding of the nature and practice of the local church surely blossomed.

There was, first of all, the church in *Ephesus*: so zealous for theological purity and yet growing coldly indifferent to one another.

This was followed by the church in *Smyrna*: wracked with poverty as a result of persecution and suffering, yet standing firm.

Then *Pergamum*: so full of love and compassion, but in danger of theological and moral compromise.

Thyatira was fourth: the epitome of growth and development, but overly tolerant of false teaching.

The church at *Sardis*: known throughout the world for life and love, but in reality rampant with spiritual putrefaction.

And *Philadelphia*: so small, so seemingly insignificant, yet so diligent and patient in the face of a hostile world.

He must have thought he had seen it all—until he came to Laodicea.

Laodicea was a wealthy city, perhaps the wealthiest in all of Phrygia. It was so wealthy that following a devastating earthquake in A.D. 60 the city rebuilt itself without financial aid from Rome. In the Annals (xiv.27) Tacitus wrote: "Laodicea arose from the ruins by the strength of her own resources, and with no help from us."

It was a city known not simply for its monetary success—it was a banking center—but for its linen and wool industry, especially black sheep, as well as its medical school. Probably the most famous medicinal product to come out of Laodicea was an eye ointment made from a powder produced in Phrygia.

Laodicea: self-confident, self-sufficient, seemingly well endowed. Yet, to such a church that considered itself rich and in need of nothing, our Lord says "Buy from me gold . . . so that you may be rich" (v. 18).

To a church that boasted of its textile industry, our Lord declares, "Buy from me . . . white garments so that you may clothe yourself and the shame of your nakedness may not be seen" (v. 18).

To a church that reveled in its contribution to ophthalmic medicine our Lord says, "Buy from me . . . salve to anoint your eyes, so that you may see" (v. 18).

The severity of this letter is unmistakable, as is also the absence of a single word of praise or commendation. As virtually dead as was the church in Sardis, there at least survived a small remnant. Not so Laodicea, in which no evidence of vitality or passion is found.

We don't know how or when the gospel came to Laodicea. Paul most likely never visited the church and thus it seems probable that Epaphras, servant of the Lord in Colossae, initiated the work there. But this we do know: the Laodiceans could hardly claim ignorance as an excuse for their spiritual slovenliness. Their failures were not due to ignorance or lack of opportunity.

Paul prayed often for the church in Laodicea (Col. 2:1). How can we begin to calculate the blessing of being the focus of such passionate apostolic intercession? They were privileged to receive the faithful and diligent ministry of Epaphras (Col. 4:13). And Paul went out of his way to make certain that his epistle to the Colossians be read to all in the church at Laodicea. No, if there were problems, and there most certainly were, it cannot be for lack of opportunity or insight or apostolic guidance.

As if that weren't enough, Paul even wrote a letter to the Laodiceans. He refers to it in Colossians 4:16 as "the letter from Laodicea," leading some to believe it was a letter actually written to Paul by the Laodicean church, or perhaps by its leadership, or even one of its members. But it's more likely that Paul has in mind a letter from him, currently in the possession of the Laodiceans, written to them, that he now wants read to the church in Colossae. But what letter might this be?

Some contend Paul is referring to his canonical letter to the Ephesians. However, the epistle to the Ephesians was most likely written after Colossians. I suppose someone could argue that Paul wrote Colossians 4:16 in view of his intent to write a more general epistle to the church at Ephesus, but this seems a bit far-fetched.

Another theory is that it was Paul's letter to Philemon, but this was a distinctly personal and private letter. Also, Philemon lived in Colossae, not Laodicea. I'm persuaded that Paul is referring to a letter that he himself wrote to the Laodiceans, one that obviously did not survive for inclusion in the canon of Scripture. We don't know what happened to it, but it's possible that it was destroyed in the massive earthquake that hit the region in A.D. 61. But that's only speculation.

You shouldn't be bothered by this, given the fact that Paul most likely wrote four letters to the Corinthian church, only two of which are included in our canon (see 1 Cor. 5:9–11, a reference to the letter written in A.D. 54, now lost; and 2 Cor. 2:4, 9, a reference to the letter written in the summer of A.D. 55, often called the "severe" or "tearful" letter, also now lost).

We have no idea why God chose not to preserve these and other apostolic writings for the church of subsequent generations. Evidently once they served their divinely designed function for the early church, God sovereignly arranged for their disappearance or destruction. In his infinite and gracious wisdom he determined that the content of those epistles was not essential for the life and faith of the church beyond the first century. Ultimately we must trust in divine providence and believe that God has preserved for us everything that is necessary for a life of truth and godliness.

In any case, it may well be that Laodicea's multiplied failures were regarded by our Lord as all the more egregious because of the remarkable opportunities she had. With much revelation comes much responsibility. To whom much is given, much is required.

I suppose the residents in that unusual city were, in certain respects, proud of what they had accomplished. But in regard to that which matters most, Laodicea was a disgrace. We would do well to listen carefully to what the Spirit said to this particular church.

41

Amen!

Revelation 3:14

"And to the angel of the church in Laodicea write: 'The words of **the Amen, the faithful and true witness, the beginning of God's creation.**'"

> My hope is built on nothing less,
> than Jesus' blood and righteousness.
> I dare not trust the sweetest frame,
> but wholly lean on Jesus' name.
> On Christ, the Solid Rock, I stand,
> all other ground is sinking sand,
> all other ground is sinking sand.[1]

We all sing it, but do we believe it? Admittedly, it's not easy to bank everything on Christ alone. Our souls long for rest in something immovable. Our minds cry out for certainty in an irrational and chaotic world. Our hearts yearn to feel the unshakable assurance that what we believe to be true is really, and I mean *really*, true.

Sadly, we often look in all the wrong places or put our hope in all the wrong people or try to convince ourselves that some newly conceived philosophical or scientific principle will finally and forever banish anxiety and doubt from our souls. Alas.

So, then, how can we know that what we know of God is true? Or better still, how can we be assured that what God has said he'll do, he'll do? To what or whom can we look to bring us the spiritual confidence that his purposes for us will come to pass and his promises to us will be fulfilled?

One answer is to remind ourselves of the historicity of the biblical record or perhaps the marvel of fulfilled prophecy. Others dispel their doubts by rehearsing over and again in their minds the airtight arguments for the bodily resurrection of Christ. A few appeal to the logical coherence or even the aesthetic beauty of Scripture itself. All these have their place, and I myself have been well served by reflecting on them at various times.

But there is a solid rock, as the hymn writer put it, on which I must stand before and above all other grounds of assurance. When I need confirmation of God's Word, when I long for validation of his promises, I look no farther than to Jesus himself, "the Amen, the faithful and true witness, the beginning of God's creation" (Rev. 3:14).

Note well: Jesus doesn't just say, "Amen"; he *is* "the Amen"! He himself is the validation, the ratification, the confirmation, the authentication of all that God has said and promised he will do for his children.

The word *amen* has a rich history in Scripture. As is still the case today as it was in the past, *amen* points to a strong affirmation of something that has been said or written. To say or, better still, to shout, "Amen!" was a person's way of expressing his or her agreement with the truth under consideration.

"Amen!" was the biblical way of making known, "Yes! I agree! By all means! So be it! Undoubtedly so! Yep! Absolutely!" When the people of God heard the word of God, they typically responded with "Amen" as a way of making it unmistakably clear: "We participate with you in declaring this to be so. There is an echo in our hearts to what you say. This truth reverberates loudly in our souls."

Today, when we want to express our solidarity with something said or desire to place our imprimatur on a claim, we often say, "Yes, that *resonates* with me." This is what is most often in view in several Old Testament texts. For example:

> "Cursed be anyone who dishonors his father or his mother." And all the people shall say, "Amen." (Deut. 27:16)

And Ezra opened the book in the sight of all the people, for he was above all the people, and as he opened it all the people stood. And Ezra blessed the LORD, the great God, and all the people answered, "Amen, Amen," lifting up their hands. And they bowed their heads and worshiped the LORD with their faces to the ground. (Neh. 8:5–6)

Blessed be his glorious name forever; may the whole earth be filled with his glory! Amen and Amen! (Ps. 72:19)

Blessed be the LORD, the God of Israel, from everlasting to everlasting! And let all the people say, "Amen!" Praise the LORD! (Ps. 106:48)

When we come to Revelation 3:14 this glorious declaration of affirmation is elevated even higher, for here it becomes one of the *names* of Jesus Christ himself (cf. Isa. 65:16). So much is this a reflection of his character and wholly consistent with his nature that he is properly named "the Amen."

So, what does this mean to you and me? How does it serve to heighten our confidence and deepen our assurance and drive out the doubts that so often plague us? Look closely with me at Paul's statement in 2 Corinthians 1:20. There we're told that "all the promises of God find their Yes in him. That is why it is through him that we utter our Amen to God for his glory."

Whatever God has promised to us—whether by way of covenant stipulation or stated intent, regardless of the context or time, no matter how unrealistic or far-fetched it may at first appear—will come to pass because of who Christ is and what he has done. He is the "Amen" to all God has said he will do. This is true not simply because Jesus adds his personal word of confirmation or stamps it with his seal of approval. It is true because he actually secures it and effectually brings it to pass by virtue of his death and resurrection. Whatever obstacles may have stood in the way of God's promises coming true, such as our sin and Satan's power, have been overcome by the blood of the Lamb.

Although at times growing up I was annoyed by the intrusive "Amen" shouted at selected intervals in the preacher's words, I now recognize how entirely appropriate and fitting this declaration of agreement really is. "In other words, the reason we say 'Amen' through Christ when we hear the promises of God preached or hear a prayer of longing for the promises of God to be fulfilled, is that Christ has said 'Amen' to us. He is God's 'Amen' to us. God says 'Amen' to us through Christ in the cross, and we respond with 'Amen' to God through Christ in preaching and prayer."[2]

The credibility of Christianity is Christ. Our confidence is in Christ. His identity and integrity ground our faith. His achievement at Calvary and the tomb are our only hope. When doubts assault your faith and anxieties threaten to suffocate your spirit, recall to mind that none other than Jesus himself has said, "Amen!" to all that God has promised on your behalf. May I suggest that, in response, you shout a heartfelt "Amen!" of your own.

42

Jesus, Man of Integrity

Revelation 3:14

"And to the angel of the church in Laodicea write: 'The words of the Amen, **the faithful and true witness**, the beginning of God's creation.'"

I doubt if anyone reading this meditation has been exempt from betrayal of one sort or another. One of life's most painful and disillusioning experiences is putting your confidence in someone who in turn lets you down. Perhaps you've shared something and made it perfectly clear that no one else is to know, only to have it become common knowledge by the end of the day. Or you trusted a lifelong friend to honor his commitment to you only to discover that when you needed him most, he was nowhere to be found.

Solomon was right: "Many a man proclaims his own steadfast love, but a faithful man who can find?" (Prov. 20:6). Well, I've found one. Jesus, who knows my works (Rev. 2:2, 19; 3:1, 8, 15); Jesus, the first and last (Rev. 2:8); Jesus, who wields a sharp two-edged sword (Rev. 2:12), with eyes like flaming fire and feet like burnished bronze (Rev. 2:18); this very Jesus is "the faithful and true witness" (Rev. 3:14) who can always be trusted to do the right thing and speak the right word.

I've often told people that one of my favorite books is Stephen L. Carter's *Integrity*.[3] Carter, professor of law at Yale University, has written a powerful book reminding us of the meaning of integrity and its essential role in our individual lives and in our existence as a society. Sadly, few have read it and even fewer heed its counsel.

Webster's defines *integrity* as "firm adherence to a code of . . . moral or artistic values," "incorruptibility," "the quality or state of being complete or undivided." The word used to describe its antithesis is "duplicity."

There is much truth in this description of Jesus in Revelation 3:14, but when I hear the words "faithful and true witness," I can't help but think of integrity. Jesus is a man of integrity, a friend who will always prove faithful, a counselor whose words will never prove false. Yes, this descriptive title also has in view our Lord's faithfulness to obey his Father's will and to fulfill every purpose for which he was sent. There's a sense in which "the faithful and true witness" is simply an expansion on the earlier declaration that Jesus is "the Amen" (Rev. 3:14). When he bears witness concerning the Father we can know he has provided an accurate portrait (see John 14:8–9).

But I see an extended application in this description of Jesus that points us to him as the preeminent person of integrity: faithful and true in all his dealings and all his declarations. In a word, he can be trusted!

Try to imagine a person who always honors his commitments, is never duplicitous or misleading or evasive in what he says, follows through on every promise, never fails to carry through on every obligation, passionately observes every law, is never wrong in his opinions, knows when to speak and when to remain silent, carefully avoids unedifying conversations, refuses to gossip, will always tell you what is most needful for your soul and will never utter so much as a syllable that might prove destructive or harmful. Got the picture? Now, think of Jesus.

When Jesus speaks or bears witness concerning a person or any particular state of affairs, or expresses an opinion or issues a warning, he can always be counted on for accuracy and honesty. When Jesus promises, he can always be trusted to follow through. He will never withhold from you what is needful for your spiritual growth. If he reveals something, it must be essential for your life, even if it's painful and demanding.

These seven letters have been difficult at times. Jesus has said things we've not always wanted to hear. But he has never pulled any punches. There have been no idle threats. Every promise is rock solid. Much of what he's said is painful, but it's always productive. You never have to pause upon reading a letter and wonder: "Did he really mean that? Surely he can't be serious." Trust me—he seriously meant it. Every word.

Perhaps the clearest word on *integrity* is found in Psalm 15. Although it is designed to govern our behavior and interpersonal relationships, no one more fully embodied its principles than Jesus, the "faithful and true witness."

For example, Jesus, more than anyone else, walked "blamelessly" (v. 2) in this life and never deviated from the path of righteousness. He "does what is right and speaks truth in his heart" (v. 3). Jesus never has and never will "slander with his tongue" (v. 3) nor do "evil to his neighbor" (v. 3).

One statement in particular stands out to me. According to Psalm 15:4, the person of integrity is one "who swears to his own hurt and does not change." The NIV renders it, "He keeps his oath even when it hurts." In other words, his honor is more important than his wallet. When a principle is at stake, personal reputation matters little. He is willing to make whatever material and physical sacrifices honesty might require.

Jesus, the faithful and true witness, never paused to ponder the personal consequences of his words or deeds. His behavior was dictated by principle, not pragmatism. If the truth he uttered led to persecution and slander and, ultimately, crucifixion, so be it.

As for the church at Laodicea, on whose behalf Jesus identified himself as "the Amen, the faithful and true witness," they could rest assured that he wasn't speaking harshly without cause. They weren't to take lightly or to any degree dismiss the warning he delivered. His analysis of their spiritual condition was spot on. His counsel for their recovery was infallible.

What this means for us, quite simply, is that we can and must embrace every word he has spoken and every directive he has issued, knowing that he never misleads, misspeaks, misguides, or makes mistakes.

Has Jesus, the faithful and true witness, promised forgiveness to those who confess and repent? Then rest assured that your sins are as white as snow. Has Jesus, the faithful and true witness, declared that he will never leave or forsake you? Then rest assured he is present, even now. Has Jesus, the faithful and true witness, revealed that he will cause everything to work together for the spiritual good of those who love him and are called according to his purpose? Then rest assured that he is graciously orchestrating the mess that you call your life for your ultimate edification and his eternal glory.

43

Jesus, Eternal Son of God
or
Jesus, Son of the Eternal God?

Revelation 3:14

"And to the angel of the church in Laodicea write: 'The words of the Amen, the faithful and true witness, **the beginning of God's creation.**'"

S am, are you playing theological tricks on us with that title? Come on. Does it really matter?" Well, let me put it this way: the difference between Jesus as "the eternal Son of God" and Jesus as "Son of the eternal God" is the difference between heaven and hell. Does that answer your question?

Let me illustrate with the story of two individuals who knew well the difference between these two ways of describing Jesus Christ and paid an eternal price for it.

The first is Arius (d. A.D. 337), who served as a presbyter in the church district of Baucalis in Alexandria, Egypt. Arius affirmed, among other things, that "the Son, born of the Father before all time, created and constituted in being before all ages, did not exist before He was begotten." The Son, he argued, was a creature, a product *ex nihilo* (out of nothing) of the divine will.

Since the Son is a creature, said Arius, he must have had a beginning. "We are persecuted," said Arius, "because we say the Son had a beginning whereas God [the Father] is without beginning." Hence, the Arian slogan: "There was [a time] when He [Jesus Christ] was not."

Arius referred to Jesus as *the Son of God* only as an expression of courtesy because of his superior participation in the grace of God. He worshiped the Son and prayed to him but denied his eternal deity.

The Council of Nicea in A.D. 325 spoke unmistakably to this heretical denial of the eternality of God the Son. Attached to the end of the creed was an *anathema*, which read: "But as for those who say, There was [a time] when He [the Son of God] was not, and before being born He was not, and that He came into existence out of nothing, or who assert that the Son of God is of a different hypostasis or substance, or is created, or is subject to alteration or change, these the Catholic Church anathematizes."

Arius denied that Jesus Christ was the *eternal* Son of God, and he died in his sin.

Michael Servetus, a Spanish physician who lived some twelve-hundred years after Arius, was of a similar mind. Upon his arrival in Geneva, Switzerland, in 1553, he was immediately arrested and charged with heresy. Although John Calvin preferred that he be beheaded, which, by sixteenth-century standards was regarded as a more dignified and humanitarian punishment, Servetus was burned at the stake while Calvin knelt in church praying for him.

As Servetus was being led to his death, his last words were carefully chosen: "Have mercy on me, Jesus, Son of the Eternal God," not "Jesus, Eternal Son of God." As Carter Lindberg has noted, "In that time a misplaced adjective could be fatal."[4] Of course, Servetus knew full well where to place the adjective and was careful and deliberate in making known his denial of the eternality of Jesus, the Son of God.

But if Jesus is without beginning or end, if he is the *eternal* Son of God, what did he mean when he identified himself in Revelation 3:14 as "the beginning of God's creation"? Is he saying that Arius and Servetus were right, that he was the first created being in a long line of others, like you and me, who owe their existence to God? No.

There are two possible ways of understanding our Lord's identification as "the beginning of God's creation."

Most have taken this phrase to mean that Jesus is the one from whom all creation begins, that he is its ultimate source or origin.

In other words, when Jesus describes himself as "the beginning of God's creation" he has in view much the same as did John in his Gospel when he said of Jesus, the Word, that "all things were made through him, and without him was not any thing made that was made" (John 1:3).

In Colossians 1:15 Paul describes Jesus as "the firstborn of all creation," or better still, "the firstborn *over* all creation." After all, in the next verse (Col. 1:16) Paul says that "by him all things were created" and again in verse 17 that the Son is "before" all things (cf. John 8:58). The word *firstborn* itself does not necessarily mean first in a sequence or first in time. It can also mean "first in rank" or "supreme in dignity." The point is that the Son, by virtue of being the image of God, has a preeminence and exercises a sovereignty over everything else that exists (see Ps. 89:27). The point, then, is that Jesus Christ is utterly unique, distinguished from all of creation because he is both eternally prior to it and supreme over it in the sense that he is its creator.

But there may be a better and more accurate way of understanding Jesus as "the beginning (Gk. *arche*) of God's creation." Contrary to what most have thought, this title of Christ does *not* have in view his relation to the old or original creation, but rather his relation to the new creation or the new cosmic order inaugurated by his resurrection from the dead.

Consider, for example, Paul's description of Jesus as "the beginning (Gk. *arche*), the firstborn from the dead" (Col. 1:18). His point is that he was the beginning and founder of a new humanity, a new people, by virtue of his having been the first to rise, never to die again. When God the Father raised him from the dead and glorified and exalted him to the right hand of the majesty on high, he became the firstfruits of that resurrection guaranteed for all who are united to him (cf. 1 Cor. 15:20–23; Rev. 1:17–18).

The resurrection of Jesus thus marks a new cosmic beginning. The use of the word "beginning" (*arche*) in both Colossians 1:18 and Revelation 3:14 points to "Christ's sovereign position in the new age."[5] Thus we see that the description of our Lord in Revelation 1:5 as "the firstborn of the dead, and the ruler of kings on earth" is "interpreted in 3:14 as designating Christ as the sovereign inaugurator of the new creation. Consequently, the title 'beginning of the creation of God' refers not to Jesus' sovereignty over the original creation but to his resurrection as demonstrating that he is the *inauguration* of and *sovereign* over the new creation."[6] Therefore, "John has in mind not Jesus as the principle, origin, or source of the original creation, but Jesus as the inaugurator of the new creation."[7]

Regardless of which view is correct, of this we may be sure: *Jesus Christ is the eternal Son of God, the uncreated creator of all things.* As such he is sovereign Lord over all of creation, both the old and the new. To believe anything less of him is to abandon all hope of eternal life.

44

Hot, Cold, or Lukewarm?

Revelation 3:15–16

"I know your works: you are neither cold nor hot. Would that you were either cold or hot! So, because you are lukewarm, and neither hot nor cold, I will spit you out of my mouth."

I doubt one could find words any more confusing and controversial than those uttered by Jesus in Revelation 3:15–16 to the church at Laodicea. Christians have expressed either befuddlement or revulsion, and sometimes both, at what our Lord says to this wayward congregation. Look at it again: "I know your works: you are neither cold nor hot. Would that you were either cold or hot! So, because you are lukewarm, and neither hot nor cold, I will spit you out of my mouth" (Rev. 3:15–16).

It makes perfectly good sense that Jesus would prefer the Laodiceans (and all of us) to be hot rather than lukewarm. But how could he possibly say that being lukewarm is worse than being cold? Doesn't this put Jesus in the position of affirming the indifferent pagan over the backslidden, halfhearted Christian? Granted, the latter is bad, but is it really the case that Jesus would prefer his lukewarm people to be in blatant unbelief?

Then there is the rather revolting image of Jesus spitting the Laodicean church out of his mouth. The marginal reference in the NASB indicates that "vomit" is actually the more literal meaning of this word. Notwithstanding the numerous threats of discipline and judgment throughout these seven letters, there's something about

Jesus being sickened to the point of vomiting his people out of his mouth that strikes us as uncharacteristically unseemly.

Our Lord's diagnosis of the problem in Laodicea is twofold. He first discerns a moral and religious tepidity in the church, a lukewarmness that borders on outright indifference to the things of God and a life of godliness. Second, he traces this to a prideful self-sufficiency (v. 17), a problem we'll address in a later meditation. So let's begin by trying to make sense of his language.

To come straight to the point, Christianity at Laodicea was flabby and anemic. Our Lord uses the language of cold, hot, and lukewarm. What does he mean by this?

As I said earlier, people have typically believed that by "hot" Jesus is referring to zealous, lively, passionate, hard-working Christians, and by "cold" he is referring to unregenerate pagans, devoid of any spiritual life whatsoever. *Hot*, so goes the argument, refers to spiritually active believers whereas *cold* refers to apathetic unbelievers. But as I said, this creates the problem of Jesus appearing to say he would rather they be in utter unbelief than in a backslidden, albeit still saved, condition.

The key to making sense of this comes from an understanding of certain features of the topography of the land in which the Laodiceans found themselves.

We must remember that Laodicea was only six miles south of Hierapolis and eleven miles west of Colossae. These three cities were the most important of all in the Lycus Valley. Laodicea itself lacked a natural water supply and was dependent on its neighbors for this vital resource. This, I believe, explains the imagery in this remarkable passage.

In all likelihood, "hot" and "cold" don't refer to the spiritual temperature or religious mood or attitude, as it were, of the believer and the unbeliever, as has traditionally been thought. Rather, the word "hot" refers to the well-known medicinal waters of Hierapolis, where hot springs reached 95 degrees. The word "cold," on the other hand, points to the refreshing waters of Colossae.

If this is what Jesus had in mind, "the church is not being called to task for its spiritual temperature but for the *barrenness* of its works."[8] The church was providing neither refreshment for the spiritually weary, portrayed through the imagery of cold water from Colossae, nor healing for the spiritually sick, portrayed through the imagery of hot water from Hierapolis. The church was simply ineffective and thus distasteful to the Lord.

If correct, this relieves the problem of why Christ would prefer the church to be cold rather than lukewarm. The church in Laodicea is rebuked, therefore, for the useless and barren nature of its works, indicative of its stagnant spiritual condition. "You've become of no benefit to anyone," says Jesus, "and I will not stomach such behavior."

One doesn't like to think of professing Christians on whose hearts Jesus rests lightly, but the Laodiceans fit the bill. This isn't to say they weren't a passionate people, only that the focus of their dedication was something other than the Lord Jesus Christ. They probably burned with desire, just not for him.

The topography of the region also sheds light on his use of the word *lukewarm*. This is probably another allusion to the hot springs of Hierapolis, located just six miles north of Laodicea. As the hot, mineral-laden waters traveled across the plateau towards Laodicea, they gradually became lukewarm before cascading over the edge directly in view of the Laodicean populace.

There are actually archaeological remains in Laodicea of an aqueduct system that would have carried water from Hierapolis. The people in Laodicea would have been keenly aware of the nauseating effect of drinking from that source.

"That is what you are like to me," says Jesus. "When I look upon your lack of zeal, your indifference toward the needs of others, and your blasé response to my beauty, I feel like a man who has over imbibed on tepid, tasteless water." It's difficult to rid one's mind of the picture of Jesus lifting to his lips a cup of what he anticipates to be a flavorful and refreshing drink, only to regurgitate it in wholesale disgust.

Does the spitting, spewing, and vomiting of such people from his mouth suggest that all hope is lost for their salvation and enjoyment of eternal fellowship with Christ? Not necessarily. This imagery, at minimum, indicates a serious threat of divine discipline. But there may yet be hope through repentance and obedience (cf. v. 19; more on this later).

In keeping with the vivid language of this text, will you join me in the following prayer? "Oh, precious Christ Jesus, the Amen, the faithful and true witness, fill me to overflowing with the sin-killing grace of your Spirit. Draw near and shatter any complacency in my soul. May my life be a fragrant aroma in your nostrils, a melodious symphony in your hearing, a beautiful sight in your eyes, a pleasing touch to your hand, and a sweet taste in your mouth! By your grace and for your glory, may my life bring refreshment to the weary soul and healing to the spiritually sick. Preserve me from lukewarm indifference. Deliver me from presumption and pride. Amen."

45

God Glorified in Man's Dependence

Revelation 3:17

"You say, I am rich, I have prospered, and I need nothing, not realizing that you are wretched, pitiable, poor, blind, and naked."

On July 8, 1731, twenty-seven-year-old Jonathan Edwards preached in Boston, Massachusetts, what would become the first of his sermons to be published. Entitled *God Glorified in Man's Dependence*, it was based on 1 Corinthians 1:29–31, a passage in which Paul was concerned that "no human being might boast in the presence of God. He," wrote Paul, "is the source of your life in Christ Jesus, whom God made our wisdom and our righteousness and sanctification and redemption. Therefore, as it is written, 'Let the one who boasts, boast in the Lord.'"[9]

All the good that we have, said Edwards, is in and through Christ. It is through him alone that true wisdom is imparted to the mind. It is by being in him that we are justified, have our sins pardoned, and are received as righteous into God's favor. Through utter dependence on Christ alone we have true excellency of heart and understanding and our actual deliverance or redemption from all misery, as well as the bestowal of all happiness and glory.

This text, he continued, reveals our "absolute and universal dependence" on God. In everything we are "directly, immediately, and entirely dependent on God." We are "dependent on him for all, and are dependent on him [in] every way." He is the ultimate *cause* for whatever good we have. He is the medium through which this good is imparted to us. And he is the good itself that is given and conveyed.

Evidently one of the primary problems in Laodicea is that they were largely oblivious to this truth. They had little sense of their utter dependence on God and proudly claimed to be spiritually rich, prosperous, and without need, all because of their own effort and self-sustaining achievement. They were living self-deluded lives, unaware of their true spiritual condition and out of touch with the source of all good.

Why was it so important for the Laodiceans to understand their spiritual plight? Why was Jesus so concerned that the blinders of self-deception and self-sufficiency be stripped away and that they see and sense their utter and absolute dependence on him for all they are and have?

The answer is simply that God will not tolerate any attitude in us or activity by us that in any way detracts from his glory. There are countless passages that bear witness to this truth, but a few will suffice.

"I am the LORD; that is my name; my glory I give to no other." (Isa. 42:8)

"My glory I will not give to another." (Isa. 48:11b)

But we have this treasure in jars of clay, to show that the surpassing power belongs to God and not to us. (2 Cor. 4:7)

As each has received a gift, use it to serve one another, as good stewards of God's varied grace . . . in order that in everything God may be glorified through Jesus Christ. (1 Pet. 4:10–11)

The self-sufficient, self-congratulatory, self-aggrandizing, self-promoting pomp and pride of the Laodiceans was not something Jesus would long tolerate. No one—not the Laodiceans, not you or I, or the most magnificent mega-church on the earth—will be permitted to detract from God's glory or take credit for what he has accomplished.

Tragically, the Laodiceans had grown plump and proud of themselves, blind to their desperate need for what only Christ can supply. "For you say, I am rich, I have prospered, and I need nothing, not realizing that you are wretched, pitiable, poor, blind, and naked" (Rev. 3:17).

George Eldon Ladd puts his finger on the problem:

> The church boasted that it was healthy and prosperous. The Greek of this verse literally rendered is, "I am rich and I have gotten riches." Not only did the church boast in her supposed spiritual well-being; she boasted that she had acquired her wealth by her own efforts. Spiritual complacency was accompanied by spiritual pride. No doubt part of her problem was the inability to distinguish between material and spiritual prosperity. The church that is prosperous materially and outwardly can easily fall into the self-deception that her outward prosperity is the measure of her spiritual prosperity.... [The church] is in reality like a blind beggar, destitute, clad in rags.[10]

Our Lord's use of terms in this passage points to a deliberate contrast on his part between the church at Smyrna and that of Laodicea. Smyrna suffered from material poverty (*ptocheia*) but was regarded by Jesus as spiritually wealthy (*plousios*). Laodicea, on the other hand, was materially wealthy (*plousios*) but spiritually poor (*ptocheia*). Thus, despite their banks, the Laodiceans were beggars. Despite their famous eye-salve, they were blind. Despite their prosperous clothing factories, they were naked.

Part of what it means to be spiritually lukewarm is to be smug, complacent, satisfied with the spiritual status quo, at rest with one's progress in the Christian life, with little or no self-awareness, little or no recognition that all is of God and his Christ.

To be lukewarm is to live as if what you presently know and experience of Christ is enough. No need or desire to press in further. No need or desire to seek after God. Little or no longing to pray and fast. Little or no longing to break free of sin. Satisfied with the current depth of delight in the Spirit. Satisfied with the current extent of knowledge of the Father. The Laodiceans were content with life as it was and not in the least ashamed or hesitant to take full credit for what little they had achieved.

If I may again use Edwardsian language, the Laodiceans felt little sense of dependence on God and thus were poised to deprive him of the praise of which he is always and ever due. And Jesus simply won't have it.

They took stock in their spiritual assets and evaluated their religious portfolio and felt rich and prosperous and in need of nothing, not even what God might give. Our Lord's assessment was of another sort. "You're spiritually bankrupt," he said, "and morally wretched and visually impaired and shamefully exposed. You have no grasp of your utter dependence on me for life and forgiveness and hope and joy and understanding and righteousness."

Edwards concluded his sermon with these words, and with them I close:

> Let us be exhorted to exalt God alone, and ascribe to him all the glory of redemption. Let us endeavor to obtain, and increase in, a sensibleness of our great dependence on God, to have our eye to him alone, to mortify a self-dependent and self-righteous disposition. Man is naturally exceedingly prone to exalt himself, and depend on his own power or goodness, as though from himself he must expect happiness. He is prone to have respect to enjoyments alien from God and his Spirit, as those in which happiness is to be found. . . . [Rather] let him give God all the glory, who alone makes him to differ from the worst of men in this world, or the most miserable of the damned in hell. Hath any man much comfort and strong hope of eternal life, let not his hope lift him up, but dispose him the more to abase himself, to reflect on his own exceeding unworthiness of such a favor, and to exalt God alone.[11]

46

Come, Ye Sinners,
Poor and Needy

Revelation 3:18

"I counsel you to buy from me gold refined by fire, so that you may be rich, and white garments so that you may clothe yourself and the shame of your nakedness may not be seen, and salve to anoint your eyes, so that you may see."

I f Jesus is in fact "the Amen, the faithful and true witness," wisdom would demand that we heed his counsel. If he can be counted on not only to confirm God's purposes ("Amen") but to speak truth without equivocation ("the faithful and true witness"), we ignore him to our peril. To casually dismiss his evaluation of the state of our souls or turn a deaf ear to his advice on how we might find healing and hope is more than morally reprehensible; it borders on insanity.

Our Lord has spoken to the Laodiceans (and to us!) without pulling any spiritual punches. He's come straight to the point in identifying the problem: a prideful, pompous, inflated sense of self-sufficiency that breeds self-delusion and lukewarm ineffectiveness.

But there's still hope, if only they'll listen and learn from "what the Spirit says to the churches." Says Jesus:

"I counsel you to buy from me gold refined by fire, so that you may
be rich, and white garments so that you may clothe yourself and the
shame of your nakedness may not be seen, and salve to anoint your
eyes, so that you may see." (Rev. 3:18)

Lukewarm professing Christians, though poor and bereft of spiritual resources, can still cash in on the only currency that counts, now
and in eternity: pure gold, refined by Jesus himself.

Those plagued by moral nakedness and the shame of exposure
can yet be adorned in clothing that may not qualify as fashion in
today's world but is more than adequate to provide covering and a
standing before a God who sees through every outward façade.

And those blinded by a false sense of self-importance, who fancy
themselves enlightened and on the cutting edge, may yet submit
to an ophthalmic physician whose healing salve strips the scales
from our darkened vision and brings clarity of sight to behold the
beauty of the King.

Continuing to draw on imagery derived from their own commercial activities, Jesus counsels them to make several purchases in
those areas where they fancy themselves self-sufficient. He likens
himself to a merchant who visits the city to sell his wares and com-
petes with other salesmen. "I advise you," he says, "to forsake your
former suppliers and come trade with me."

True spiritual wealth, the sort that cannot rust or be stolen or
suffer from a Wall Street crash or plummeting interest rates, is the
gold that is purified of all dross and rid of every alloy by the refining
fires of suffering (cf. Job 23:10; Prov. 27:21; Mal. 3:2–3; 1 Pet. 1:6–9).
This is the gold of knowing Christ, enjoying Christ, savoring Christ,
treasuring Christ, prizing Christ, and finding in him alone the fullness
of joy that will never fade or lose its capacity to please.

There is an obvious paradox here, for how can poor people purchase a commodity as expensive as gold? You do so with the only
currency that counts in God's presence: need. The coin of the realm
is desperation. We don't pay him out of our resources but from an
acknowledgment of the depths of our abject poverty. The price
God requires is that faith in him that humbly concedes that one has
nothing with which to bargain, nothing with which to trade, nothing
with which to make so much as a meager down payment.

Here, then, is the good, great, and glorious news to the "poor in spirit" (Matt. 5:3):

"Come, everyone who thirsts, come to the waters; and he who has no money, come, buy and eat! Come, buy wine and milk without money and without price. Why do you spend your money for that which is not bread, and your labor for that which does not satisfy? Listen diligently to me, and eat what is good, and delight yourselves in rich food." (Isa. 55:1–2)

The Laodiceans were desperately and embarrassingly lacking those garments the fabric of which covers all sin and clothes all nakedness, whose "style" alone counts in the presence of God. We live in a world shamefully accustomed to praising the self-absorbed actress who primps publicly in the latest Versace gown. But on the final day, only those clothed in the Son will withstand the scrutiny of him whose eye is turned not toward the fleeting fashion of human achievement but to the moral substance of conformity to Christ alone.

For people living in first-century Laodicea, the imagery would have evoked an unmistakable contrast in their minds between the famous and profitable black wool from the sheep in Laodicea and the white woolen garments essential to their spiritual lives.

Finally, they are desperately in need of the restoration of their spiritual vision. The founder of the medical school at Laodicea was a famous ophthalmologist named Demosthenes Philalethes. As helpful as his remedies might be for the physical eye, only Jesus can apply that soothing, healing, restorative salve that enables us to behold and enjoy beauty that never fades or fails. John Stott's words are to the point:

Here is welcome news for naked, blind beggars! They are poor; but Christ has gold. They are naked; but Christ has clothes. They are blind; but Christ has eyesalve. Let them no longer trust in their banks, their Phrygian eyepowders and their clothing factories. Let them come to Him! He can enrich their poverty, clothe their nakedness and heal their blindness. He can open their eyes to perceive a spiritual world of which they have never dreamed. He can cover their sin and shame and make them fit to partake of the inheritance of the saints in light. He can enrich them with life and life abundant.[12]

217

Hymn writer Joseph Hart captured the essence of our Lord's appeal, whether it be to the Laodiceans then or to the church, any church, today:

> Come, ye sinners, poor and needy,
> Weak and wounded, sick and sore;
> Jesus ready stands to save you,
> Full of pity, love and power.
>
> Come, ye thirsty, come, and welcome,
> God's free bounty glorify;
> True belief and true repentance,
> Every grace that brings you nigh.
>
> View Him prostrate in the garden;
> On the ground your Maker lies.
> On the bloody tree behold Him;
> Sinner, will this not suffice?
>
> Lo! th'incarnate God ascended,
> Pleads the merit of His blood.
> Venture on Him, venture wholly,
> Let no other trust intrude.
>
> Let not conscience make you linger,
> Not of fitness fondly dream;
> All the fitness He requireth
> Is to feel your need of Him.

47

When Love Hurts

Revelation 3:19

"Those whom I love, I reprove and discipline, so be zealous and repent."

R evelation 3:19 is nothing short of shocking. Earlier in verse 16 Jesus expressed disgust towards those in Laodicea, declaring that he is on the verge of vomiting them out of his mouth. Yet now, in verse 19, he affirms his love for them. May I boldly suggest that it is precisely because he loves his people that he refuses to tolerate their lukewarm indifference toward spiritual matters? In other words, the harsh words in this letter, the firm discipline evoked by their backslidden behavior, together with the strong counsel (v. 18) that they "be zealous and repent" (v. 19) are all motivated by our Lord's love for his own.

If you're looking for an explanation of our Lord's posture in relation to Laodicea, you need go no farther than Revelation 3:19. He says and does what we read in this letter because of his loving commitment to them. "Those whom I love, I reprove and discipline, so be zealous and repent" (Rev. 3:19). If this passage is to make sense to us we need to understand something about the nature of divine discipline.[13]

Although it sounds good, pain-free Christianity is a contradiction in terms. It doesn't exist except in the deceptive sermons of some advocates of the health-and-wealth gospel. If you want to be told that living for Jesus holds forth the potential for ease and comfort and opulence, there is no shortage of preachers and teachers who will be only too happy to oblige you. They live for the opportunity to tickle your ears with promises of no sickness and no suffering for those in whom there is no sin.

The appeal of this false gospel is self-evident. Who wouldn't want the best of everything with no discomfort, no disabilities, no distress? After all, we're not masochists! I'm not at all shocked that the prosperity gospel has such a vast and enthusiastic following. When people crave prosperity you can rest assured they'll flock like geese to the side of whoever it is that's making the offer.

But there's no escaping the fact that sometimes love hurts. I don't mean that it hurts because we love someone who fails to love us back, although, of course, that's often true. I'm talking about God's love. Sometimes, because God is love, you will hurt.

Consider the words of Solomon in Proverbs 3:11–12, the passage to which Jesus obviously alludes in Revelation 3:19: "My son, do not despise the LORD's discipline or be weary of his reproof, for the LORD reproves him whom he loves, as a father the son in whom he delights." An expanded commentary on Solomon's counsel is found in Hebrews 12:5–11:

> Have you forgotten the exhortation that addresses you as sons? "My son, do not regard lightly the discipline of the Lord, nor be weary when reproved by him. For the Lord disciplines the one he loves, and chastises every son whom he receives." It is for discipline that you have to endure. God is treating you as sons. For what son is there whom his father does not discipline? If you are left without discipline, in which all have participated, then you are illegitimate children and not sons. Besides this, we have had earthly fathers who disciplined us and we respected them. Shall we not much more be subject to the Father of spirits and live? For they disciplined us for a short time as it seemed best to them, but he disciplines us for our good, that we may share his holiness. For the moment all discipline seems painful rather than pleasant, but later it yields the peaceful fruit of righteousness to those who have been trained by it.

The pain of divine discipline is the proof of your Father's passionate love. Contrary to what many child psychologists and not a few theologians have argued, "discipline is the mark not of a harsh and heartless father but of a father who is deeply and lovingly concerned for the well-being of his son."[14]

"If I am God's child, why does he allow me to suffer?" is an absurd and inappropriate question. It is *because* you are his child, dear and precious to his heart, that he cleanses and educates you with various trials.

The discipline in view in Hebrews 12 is likely the sort that is provoked by our sin. When we wander or stray from the path of purity, our loving Father chastens us, whether with physical distress, trials, or other forms of pain. Our author's point is that, far from a sign of God's hatred or indifference toward us, his love demands it.

To sin with impunity may at first strike you as attractive until you realize that it serves only to reveal that you are still a spiritual orphan. If you are God's child, you will receive his discipline. If God loves you, chastening is inevitable.

I've known people who, when they were young, envied friends whose parents were given to lax, often nonexistent, discipline. They lamented the strict and frequently painful measures their own parents imposed, especially during the years of adolescent immaturity and rebellion. But what may at the time have seemed like the ideal father or mother now appears to be a tragic expression of loveless and indifferent neglect.

I wouldn't say this if it weren't for the fact that the author of Hebrews says it. So here goes. To go through life pain free, void of discipline, is to be a spiritual bastard (cf. Heb. 12:8). A life free of hardship signals that you are no child of God. Rejoice, therefore, in your distress, for it proves you have a Father who cares enough to chasten.

Whereas it is true that the discipline in view here is provoked by disobedience, that isn't always the case. There are lessons in the Christian life that cannot be learned apart from a rigorous and often painful process. God's love does not always provide us with a quick fix or an easy out. It isn't for lack of love that we are frequently left to struggle and fall and suffer both physical and spiritual injury. Sometimes love requires it.

Paul learned this from his thorn in the flesh. However you choose to interpret the thorn, one thing is clear: the discomfort it inflicted was essential to his holiness. He wasn't being punished because of his sin. Rather, the thorn was God's device for keeping him from it: "To keep me from becoming conceited . . . a thorn was given me in the flesh" (2 Cor. 12:7).

J. I. Packer encourages us to think of this in terms of the training of children. He points out what every parent certainly knows, namely, that if "there are never any difficult situations that demand self-denial and discipline, if there are never any sustained pressures to cope with, if there are never any long-term strategies where the child must stick with an educational process, or an apprenticeship, or the practice of a skill, for many years in order to advance, there will never be any maturity of character."[15]

Our children may beg to differ. But if we cater to their demands in this regard they will grow up soft and spoiled, because everything will have been made too easy for them. Our heavenly Father, on the other hand, will never allow that to happen in the lives of his children.

The final lesson to learn about God's chastening love is that although painful, it is always profitable. "For the moment all discipline seems painful rather than pleasant," writes the author of Hebrews, "but later it yields the peaceful fruit of righteousness to those who have been trained by it" (Heb. 12:11).

In other words, pain hurts! But it's also helpful. God doesn't expect us to grit our teeth and deny that trials are troublesome. He knows the discomfort we feel in body and soul. He also knows that occasionally there simply is no other, or at least no better, way of cultivating holiness in the stubborn soil of our souls.

The next time you're hurting and tempted to question God's love for you, recall these texts: Proverbs 3:11–12; Hebrews 12:5-11; and Revelation 3:19. Remind yourself that the measure of true love is the pursuit of righteousness in the beloved. God permits us to hurt because he is passionately committed to making us holy. There is no love in providing comfort to someone in sin.

I assume that if you were suffering from a recurring pain in your head, you would seek the advice and assistance of your family physician. Suppose he suggested that a couple of aspirin would suffice to eliminate the pain, knowing that its cause was in fact a malignant tumor? Your outrage would be wholly justified.

But what if he responded by saying: "I wanted to tell you the truth but I knew how sad it would make you feel. I knew how painful it would be for you to undergo the required operation. I knew how much of an inconvenience and financial expense it would prove to be, so I thought it would be more loving if I wrote it off as just another headache."

My guess is that, notwithstanding his expression of love, you would be seriously tempted to sue for malpractice. If this doctor really cared for you, he would have taken whatever steps necessary to preserve your life, even if those steps proved painful. Likewise, our Father often has to perform a little spiritual surgery to excise the tumor of sin and rebellion and unbelief. It hurts, it's confusing, it's inconvenient, but above all else it's loving.

It was a hard lesson for the Laodiceans to learn. Whether or not they eventually grasped this truth and did what Jesus commanded— "be zealous and repent" (see the subsequent meditation)—remains a mystery. The only remaining and relevant question is whether *we* will embrace the discipline of our loving Lord and run to him, rather than from him, when we sin.

48

Be Zealous and Repent

Revelation 3:19

"Those whom I love, I reprove and discipline, so **be zealous and repent**."

The foundation for a relationship of passion is a heart of purity. *Sin kills intimacy*. It comes as no surprise, then, that perhaps the greatest obstacle to a vibrant and intimate relationship with Jesus Christ is the failure or refusal to repent. This accounts for our Lord's pointed plea to the Laodiceans: "Be zealous and repent" (Rev. 3:19).

What, exactly, did Jesus have in mind when he called the Laodiceans (and us) to a zealous, immediate, unqualified repentance? What is repentance? I want to portray repentance in terms of five realities.[16]

First of all, it begins with *recognition*, which is to say, an eye-opening, heart-rending awareness of having defied God by embracing what he despises and despising, or at minimum, being indifferent toward, what he adores. Repentance, therefore, involves confessing from the heart: "This is wrong"; "I have sinned"; "God is grieved."

The antithesis of recognition is rationalization, the pathetic attempt to justify one's moral laxity by any number of appeals: "I'm a victim! You have no idea what I've been through. If you knew how rotten my life has been and how badly people have treated me, you'd give me a little slack."

True repentance, notes J. I. Packer, "only begins when one passes out of what the Bible sees as *self-deception* (cf. James 1:22, 26; 1 John 1:8) and modern counselors call *denial*, into what the Bible calls *conviction of sin* (cf. John 16:8)."[17]

We must remember that "confession by itself is not repentance. Confession moves the lips; repentance moves the heart. Naming an act as evil before God is not the same as leaving it. Though your confession may be honest and emotional, it is not enough unless it expresses a true change of heart. There *are* those who confess only for the show of it, whose so-called repentance may be theatrical but not actual."[18]

The second element in repentance is *remorse*. If one is not genuinely offended by one's sin, there is no repentance. Repentance is painful, but it is a sweet pain. It demands brokenness of heart (Ps. 51:17; Isa. 57:15) but always with a view to healing and restoration and a renewed vision of the beauty of Christ and forgiving grace.

Repentance is more than a feeling. Emotion can be fleeting, whereas true repentance bears fruit. This points to the difference between attrition and contrition. *Attrition* is regret for sin prompted by a fear for oneself: "Oh, no. I got caught. What will happen to me?" *Contrition*, on the other hand, is regret for the offense against God's love and pain for having grieved the Holy Spirit. In other words, it is possible to "repent" out of fear of reprisal, rather than from a hatred of sin.

Paul had this distinction in mind when he wrote 2 Corinthians 7:6–11. Due to the insidious influence of a group of false teachers who were undermining his apostolic authority in Corinth, as well as for other reasons, the apostle was forced to write what he calls a sorrowful letter to the church in that city. Paul initially regretted causing them grief by this letter but later rejoiced when he saw the fruit in their lives that the letter produced. "As it is," said Paul, "I rejoice, not because you were grieved, but because you were grieved into repenting. For you felt a godly grief, so that you suffered no loss through us. For godly grief produces a repentance that leads to salvation without regret, whereas worldly grief produces death. For see what earnestness this godly grief has produced in you, but also what eagerness to clear yourselves, what indignation, what fear, what longing, what zeal, what punishment! At every point you have proved yourselves innocent in the matter" (vv. 9–11).

Paul speaks of godly grief in verse 9 and the godly repentance it produces in verse 10. Godly grief or sorrow is the sort that is agreeable to the mind and will of God; sorrow prompted by recognition that one's sin has offended God. Worldly grief (v. 10) is born of self-pity and anger for being exposed. The test that distinguishes the two is simple: does your sorrow lead to repentance?

In the case of the Corinthians the fruit of godly repentance is unmistakable: earnestness to do what was right; vindication of themselves, not in denying they had done wrong (vv. 9–10) but in being roused to a concern for their reputation lest they bring reproach on Christ and the gospel; indignation with themselves for having allowed the situation to develop as it did; fear of God and of Paul (see 1 Cor. 4:21); longing, as in verse 7, to be reunited; zeal for Paul (v. 7); punishment or the avenging of wrong, i.e., their desire to see that justice is done by bringing the guilty person(s) to discipline.

Paul's statement that such repentance leads to salvation (v. 10) points to the fact that "the nature of their response to Paul's letter was in itself a sure indication that they were, as they professed to be, genuine Christians, and not dissemblers [i.e., hypocritical pretenders]."[19]

Remorse, regret, sorrow, and the pain provoked by sin will only increase and intensify the longer we are Christians. Maturity in the faith does not lead to less sorrow over sin, but more. The pain does not diminish; it deepens. Says Packer: "It is, in fact, a law of the spiritual life that the further you go, the more you are aware of the distance still to be covered. Your growing desire for God makes you increasingly conscious, not so much of where you are in your relationship with him as of where as yet you are not."[20]

The third essential element in real repentance is *request*. We must *ask* God for forgiveness and for strength. In David's repentant prayer in Psalm 51, we see both his request for forgiveness (vv. 7–9) and his request for strength and renewal (vv. 10–12).

Fourth, there must be *repudiation* of all sins in question and active practical steps taken to avoid anything that might provoke stumbling (cf. Acts 19:18–19). In other words, there must be a deliberate resolve to turn around and away from all hint or scent of sin (Ps.

139:23). Paul writes: "But put on the Lord Jesus Christ, and make no provision for the flesh, to gratify its desires" (Rom. 13:14). If, in our so-called repentance, we do not abandon the environment in which our sin first emerged and in which, in all likelihood, it will continue to flourish, our repentance is suspect.

Finally, there must be heartfelt *reformation*, which is to say, an overt determination to pursue purity, to do what pleases God (1 Thess. 1:9). For the Laodiceans this meant forsaking whatever might perpetuate the spiritual sluggishness and unwarranted self-sufficiency in which they languished.

Perhaps the best place for each of us to begin is with the sentiments expressed in this hymn:

> Search me, O God, my actions try,
>   And let my life appear
> As seen by thine all-searching eye;
>   To mine my ways make clear.
>
> Search all my sense and know my heart,
>   Who only canst make known,
> And let the deep, the hidden part
>   To me be fully shown.
>
> Throw light into the darkened cells
>   Where passion reigns within;
> Quicken my conscience till it feels
>   The loathsomeness of sin.
>
> Search all my thoughts, the secret springs,
>   The motives that control,
> The chambers where polluted things
>   Hold empire o'er the soul.

49

Intimacy in the Inner Room

Revelation 3:20

"Behold, I stand at the door and knock. If anyone hears my voice and opens the door, I will come in to him and eat with him, and he with me."

Next to John 3:16, this is perhaps the most famous evangelistic passage in the New Testament. The question is, should it be? To this lukewarm and backslidden church, Jesus issues this stunning invitation: "Behold, I stand at the door and knock. If anyone hears my voice and opens the door, I will come in to him and eat with him, and he with me" (Rev. 3:20).

As noted, most people simply assume this is an evangelistic appeal to non-Christians to open the door of their hearts and invite Jesus in to save and forgive them. Let me say first of all that if you came to saving faith in Christ in response to the use of this passage in an evangelistic presentation, praise God! The fact that this text was, in all likelihood, used in a way inconsistent with its original intent in no way invalidates the spiritual life God graciously imparted to you through it.

There's one more thing to note before we proceed. Colin Hemer has pointed out that Jesus has once again drawn on imagery familiar to the people of Laodicea in order to make his point, for the city was situated foursquare on one of the most important road junctions in Asia Minor. Each of the four city gates opened on to a busy trade route. The inhabitants of Laodicea, therefore, "must have been very familiar with the belated traveler who 'stood at the door and knocked' for admission."[21]

According to the most commonly held view, this appeal by Jesus is addressed to unbelievers. The door at which Christ stands is the door to one's heart or life. The knocking and voice of Christ are heard through the preaching of the gospel. The opening of the door is the decision of the will to invite Christ into one's heart or life. The result is that in conversion Christ enters the person to take up permanent residence.

Another, more likely view, is that the invitation is addressed to backslidden, unrepentant believers who, in their self-sufficiency, had excluded (indeed, excommunicated) the risen Lord from their congregational and personal lives. But in an expression of indescribable condescension and love Jesus asks permission to enter and reestablish fellowship with his people, a fellowship portrayed in the imagery of a feast in which Christ and Christians share.

One final view to consider is eschatological in nature. This interpretation says that the invitation (v. 20) has a *future* fulfillment. It is addressed to backslidden believers in the church at Laodicea and pertains to Christ's second coming. The door at which Jesus stands is a metaphor for the imminence of his return (cf. James 5:9). Those who are prepared and alert to receive their Savior at his coming will enjoy intimate communion with him in the messianic feast of the age to come. This view links verse 20 with verse 21 and the promise of co-regency in the future kingdom.

The salvation view strikes me as highly unlikely. According to verse 19, Jesus is addressing the children of God who, as children, are recipients of divine, loving discipline. Jesus has in view the corporate discipline of the church, similar to what we saw in Revelation 2:5 with regard to the church at Ephesus.

Also, verse 19, as noted in an earlier meditation, is an obvious allusion to Proverbs 3:11–12 and Hebrews 12:5–6, both of which have in view the children of God. We should also note the connection between verse 19 and verse 20, the latter being a description of what repentance is and what follows upon it, namely, a restoration of intimate communion between Jesus and the believer. We also must acknowledge the obvious reference to the messianic kingdom feast (in this regard, see Luke 12:35–39; 22:28–30). Added to this is the fact that the sharing of table fellowship was a common image in those days for deep communion and the strong bonds of affection and companionship.

Whereas some see in the "feast" and the imagery of dining a reference to the Lord's Supper, or Eucharist, I find this unlikely. The picture here is one in which Jesus himself dines personally with the individual, whereas in the Eucharist it is we all, corporately, who share a meal in remembrance of the sacrifice of Christ.

Thus the appeal of verse 20 is not to unbelievers so that they might be saved. Rather it is an appeal to individuals ("anyone") within the church to repent and forsake their spiritual half-heartedness. As a result one may experience now the intimate communion and fellowship of which the feast in the messianic kingdom is the consummation. All present fellowship with Jesus is a foretaste of that eternal felicity which will be consummated in the age to come.

What, then, should be our response today to this divine invitation? I'll let John Piper answer that and conclude with his words. In agreement with the view I've suggested, Piper says:

> [This letter] is addressed to lukewarm Christians who think they have need of nothing more of Christ. It is addressed to churchgoers who do not enjoy the riches of Christ or the garments of Christ or the medicine of Christ because they keep the door shut to the inner room of their lives. All the dealings they have with Christ are businesslike lukewarm dealings with a salesman on the porch.

> But Christ did not die to redeem a bride who would keep him on the porch while she watched television in the den. His will for the church is that we open the door, all the doors of our life. He wants to join you in the dining room, spread a meal out for you, and eat with you and talk with you. *The opposite of lukewarmness is the fervor you experience when you enjoy a candlelit dinner with Jesus Christ in the innermost room of your heart.* And when Jesus Christ, the source of all God's creation, is dining with you in your heart, then you have all the gold, all the garments, and all the medicine in the world.

> How do you buy gold when you're broke? You *pray*, and trust the promise: "I will come in to you and eat with you, and you with me." There is an intimate communion and fellowship with Christ which many of us . . . need to seek in earnest prayer. *Because when he dwells in the innermost room of our affections, he brings the power we want more than anything—the power to conquer selfishness and live for others."*[22]

50

Enthroned!

Revelation 3:21–22

"The one who conquers, I will grant him to sit with me on my throne, as I also conquered and sat down with my Father on his throne. He who has an ear, let him hear what the Spirit says to the churches."

No matter how many times I read this promise, I struggle to believe it. That's not because I doubt its inspiration or accuracy. Jesus meant what he said, and I embrace it. But to think of myself enthroned with Christ is simply more than I can fathom. Others of you may have a better grip on this than I do, but it strikes me as so utterly outlandish, not to mention presumptuous and prideful, that I blink at the words and have to pause simply to catch my breath.

This may be one of the reasons why Jesus concludes this letter, as he does each of the other six, with the exhortation to hear what he is saying to us through the Spirit. In other words, knowing the effect that such statements would have, as well as knowing our tendency toward incredulity, he had to go out of his way in every letter to reinforce the urgency of what he commands as well as the reality of what he promises.

It's as if he takes hold of my shoulders, shaking me firmly but lovingly, and says, "Sam, did you hear what I just said? Read it again. Hear it again. Turn it over in your mind, again. Don't resist the Spirit's work of imprinting this indelibly on your soul. If you overcome the temptation to capitulate to the world's invitation, if you resist the allure of lukewarm religiosity and invite me in to that spiritual room of greatest intimacy (Rev. 3:20), you will sit down with me on my throne."

Perhaps this promise would rest more easily in my heart if it weren't for the fact that Revelation 4 and 5 follow immediately on this concluding letter to the church at Laodicea. You see, when I pause to reflect on what Christ meant when he referred to his throne, a throne on which his people, together with him, will sit, I can't help but be drawn into the majestic scene that follows in the subsequent two chapters.

What we see and hear and feel in Revelation 4–5 is the pinnacle of biblical revelation. There simply is no greater, more majestic, or breathtaking scene than that of the risen Lamb sitting on the throne, surrounded by adoring angels and odd creatures, with ear-popping peals of thunder and blinding bolts of lightning.

If my earlier discomfort was due to the seeming impropriety of sinners sitting on that throne, nothing is more proper or fitting or apropos than that Jesus should be there. Nothing makes more sense than that he should be the focus of all creation, whether of elders falling down, mesmerized by his beauty, or strange animals singing endlessly of his holiness. He belongs on the throne. He alone is God! He has died and redeemed men and women from every tribe and tongue and people and nation. By all means, let us sing:

> Crown Him with many crowns, the Lamb upon His throne.
> Hark! How the heavenly anthem drowns all music but its own.
> Awake, my soul, and sing, of Him who died for thee,
> And hail Him as thy matchless King through all eternity.

Were ever more fitting words found on human lips? Yet again, we sing:

> Crown Him the Lord of Heaven, enthroned in worlds above,
> Crown Him the King to Whom is given the wondrous name of Love.
> Crown Him with many crowns, as thrones before Him fall;
> Crown Him, ye kings, with many crowns, for He is King of all.

Yes, he is the Lord of heaven (and earth) and is rightly "enthroned in worlds above." But what, for heaven's sake, if I may be permitted to use such words, are *we* doing there? There's more.

Crown Him the Lord of lords, who over all doth reign,
Who once on earth, the incarnate Word, for ransomed sinners slain,
Now lives in realms of light, where saints with angels sing,
Their songs before Him day and night, their God, Redeemer, King.

And what, for heaven's sake, will the twenty-four elders think? What will be the reaction of the four living creatures, not to mention the myriads of angelic beings who surround the throne, pouring forth wave upon wave of endless praise? Will they not be shocked and scandalized to see sinners there? I would be! One more time, we rightly sing:

Crown Him the Lord of years, the Potentate of time,
Creator of the rolling spheres, ineffably sublime.
All hail, Redeemer, hail! For Thou has died for me;
Thy praise and glory shall not fail throughout eternity.[23]

We must be very careful and theologically fastidious on this point. We are not enthroned with Christ because we *are* Christ, as if salvation entails the merging of our being with his in such a way that he is less than the Creator or that we are more than creatures. Our union with him is vital and glorious but he is always the one and only living Lord, and we are redeemed sinners who depend on him not only now but for all eternity.

We are not enthroned with him because we will have been deified, as if we will have left behind our humanity and been transformed into divinity. We will forever be monotheists, affirming and worshiping only one God who lives eternally as Father, Son, and Spirit. We are not enthroned because we are God, but because he is! Although we will be "made like him" (see 1 John 3:2; Phil. 3:21), gloriously devoid of all sinful impulses, our presence on his throne is a gift, not a right. We are there not by nature or deed but by grace alone, having been made co-heirs by him who alone is worthy of worship.

Having said all that, I'm still a bit incredulous when it comes to this promise in Revelation 3:21–22 (cf. Rev. 2:26–27). But at least I know why I'm enthroned with him and why not. I'm there because he died for me and poured out the love of God into my heart through the Spirit who was given to me (Rom. 5:5). I'm there because of mercy, not merit. I'm there to share his rule, not usurp it. I'm there to exercise an authority that is rightfully his and derivatively mine.

I don't expect ever fully to understand what this promise means or entails. Its shape is still uncertain to me. What it will feel like is yet foreign. Its plausibility confronts me like an insurmountable mountain peak. That Christ Jesus should ever make room within his reign for a scurrilous sinner like me is no doubt a theme that will occupy my thoughts and inquiries for all eternity. As for now, I don't know what else to say but, "Thank you, Lord!"

Notes

Introduction to the Seven Letters to the Seven Churches

1. George E. Ladd, *A Commentary on the Revelation of John* (Grand Rapids, MI: Eerdmans, 1976), 24.

2. William M. Ramsay, *The Letters to the Seven Churches of Asia* (Grand Rapids, MI: Baker, 1985), 178.

3. G. K. Beale, *The Book of Revelation: A Commentary on the Greek Text* (Grand Rapids, MI: Eerdmans, 1999), 226.

4. Walter Scott, *Exposition of the Revelation of Jesus Christ* (London: Pickering and Inglis, n.d.), no page ref.

5. Colin Hemer, *The Letters to the Seven Churches of Asia in Their Local Setting* (Sheffield: JSOT Press, 1986), 15.

6. Meredith Kline, "A Study in the Structure of the Revelation of John," unpublished paper, 1945.

7. Paul Minear, *I Saw a New Earth: An Introduction to the Visions of the Apocalypse* (Washington: Corpus, 1969).

8. G. K. Beale, *The Book of Revelation*, 225.

9. Ibid., 226–27.

The Church in Ephesus

1. John Stott, *What Christ Thinks of the Church* (Grand Rapids, MI: Eerdmans, 1972).

2. G. K. Beale, *The Book of Revelation: A Commentary on the Greek Text* (Grand Rapids, MI: Eerdmans, 1999), 208–9.

3. Wayne Grudem, *Systematic Theology: An Introduction to Biblical Doctrine* (Grand Rapids, MI: Zondervan, 1994), 191.

4. Carl F. H. Henry, *God, Revelation and Authority: The God Who Stands and Stays* (Dallas: Word Publishing, 1983), 5:268.

5. Charles H. Spurgeon, *The Treasury of David* (Peabody: Hendrickson, n.d.), 3:258.

6. Ibid., 259.

7. John Piper, "Savoring God by Serving the Saints," a sermon on Heb. 6:9–12, February 2, 1992, http://www.desiringgod.org.

8. Grant R. Osborne, *Revelation* (Grand Rapids, MI: Baker Academic, 2002), 115.

9. G. R. Beasley-Murray, *The Book of Revelation* (Greenwood, SC: Attic Press, 1974), 75.

10. David E. Aune, *Revelation 1–5*, Word Biblical Commentary (Dallas: Word Books, 1997), 152.

11. Ibid.

12. Colin Hemer, *The Letters to the Seven Churches of Asia in Their Local Setting* (Sheffield: JSOT Press, 1986), 41–55.

13. Ibid., 55.

The Church in Smyrna

1. George E. Ladd, *A Commentary on the Revelation of John* (Grand Rapids, MI: Eerdmans, 1976), 43–44.

2. John Stott, *What Christ Thinks of the Church* (Grand Rapids, MI: Eerdmans, 1972), 39.

3. Colin Hemer, *The Letters to the Seven Churches of Asia in Their Local Setting* (Sheffield: JSOT Press, 1986), 70.

4. John Stott, *What Christ Thinks of the Church*, 43.

5. Sydney Page, *Powers of Evil: A Biblical Study of Satan and Demons* (Grand Rapids, MI: Baker, 1995), 124.

The Church in Pergamum

1. John Stott, *What Christ Thinks of the Church* (Grand Rapids, MI: Eerdmans, 1972), 51–52 (emphasis mine).

2. Colin Hemer, *The Letters to the Seven Churches of Asia in Their Local Setting* (Sheffield: JSOT Press, 1986), 85.

3. Grant R. Osborne, *Revelation* (Grand Rapids, MI: Baker Academic, 2002), 140.

4. Charles H. Spurgeon, pub. data unavailable.

5. Jonathan Edwards, "The Miscellanies," in *The Works of Jonathan Edwards*, vol. 13, no. 182, ed. Thomas A. Schafer (New Haven: Yale University Press, 1994), 328.

6. Colin Hemer, *The Letters to the Seven Churches of Asia*, 99.

7. G. K. Beale, *The Book of Revelation: A Commentary on the Greek Text* (Grand Rapids, MI: Eerdmans, 1999), 253.

8. Colin Hemer, *The Letters to the Seven Churches of Asia*, 103–4.

The Church in Thyatira

1. John Stott, *What Christ Thinks of the Church* (Grand Rapids, MI: Eerdmans, 1972), 71.

2. John F. Walvoord, *The Revelation of Jesus Christ* (Chicago: Moody Press, 1966), 75.

3. Leon Morris, *The Revelation of St. John: An Introduction and Commentary*, rev. ed. (Grand Rapids, MI: Eerdmans, 1999), 71.

4. Robert H. Mounce, *The Book of Revelation*, rev. ed. (Grand Rapids, MI: Eerdmans, 1998 [1977]), 104.

5. For more information on this issue, I refer you to my book, *The Beginner's Guide to Spiritual Gifts* (Regal, 2002), 97–99.

6. G. R. Beasley-Murray, *The Book of Revelation* (Greenwood, SC: Attic Press, 1974), 94–95.

The Church in Sardis

1. G. R. Beasley-Murray, *The Book of Revelation* (Greenwood, SC: Attic Press, 1974), 94.

2. R. H. Charles, *A Critical and Exegetical Commentary on the Revelation of St. John* (Edinburgh: T. & T. Clark, 1975 [1920]), 1:78.

3. Ibid.

4. G. B. Caird, *A Commentary on the Revelation of St. John the Divine* (New York: Harper & Row, 1966), 48.

5. John Stott, *What Christ Thinks of the Church* (Grand Rapids, MI: Eerdmans, 1972), 85.

6. Paul Barnett, *The Second Epistle to the Corinthians* (Grand Rapids, MI: Eerdmans, 1997), 150 (final emphasis mine).

7. Ben Witherington, *Conflict and Community in Corinth: A Socio-Rhetorical Commentary on 1 and 2 Corinthians* (Grand Rapids, MI: Eerdmans, 1995), 366.

8. Ibid.

9. George E. Ladd, *A Commentary on the Revelation of John* (Grand Rapids, MI: Eerdmans, 1976), 56.

10. David E. Aune, *Revelation 1–5*, Word Biblical Commentary (Dallas: Word Books, 1997), 1:221.

11. See http://www.SamStorms.com, "Book Reviews" in the Recommended section.

12. G. K. Beale, *The Book of Revelation: A Commentary on the Greek Text* (Grand Rapids, MI: Eerdmans, 1999).

13. Colin Hemer, *The Letters to the Seven Churches of Asia in Their Local Setting* (Sheffield: JSOT Press, 1986), 148.

14. John Piper, "Can the Regenerate Be Erased from the Book of Life?" 12/22/06, http://www.desiringgod.org (emphasis in original).

15. Ibid (emphasis in original).

The Church in Philadelphia

1. Sam Storms, *Pleasures Evermore: The Life-Changing Power of Enjoying God* (Colorado Springs: NavPress, 2000).

2. David E. Aune, *Revelation 1–5*, Word Biblical Commentary (Dallas: Word Books, 1997), 1:238.

3. Michael Wilcock, *The Message of Revelation: I Saw Heaven Opened* (Downers Grove: InterVarsity, 1975), 54.

4. G. K. Beale, *The Book of Revelation: A Commentary on the Greek Text* (Grand Rapids, MI: Eerdmans, 1999), 292.

5. Ibid., 293.

6. Ibid., 295.

7. Ibid.

8. Robert H. Mounce, *The Book of Revelation*, rev. ed. (Grand Rapids, MI: Eerdmans, 1998 [1977]), 120–21.

9. H. B. Swete, *Commentary on Revelation* (Grand Rapids, MI: Kregel, 1977), 57.

The Church in Laodicea

1. Edward Mote, "The Solid Rock," 1863.

2. John Piper, "Amen," a sermon on 1 Corinthians 14:6–19, February 1, 1998, http://www.desiringgod.org.

3. Stephen L. Carter, *Integrity* (New York: Basic Books, 1996).

4. Carter Lindberg, *The European Reformations* (Cambridge: Blackwell, 1996), 269.

5. G. K. Beale, *The Book of Revelation: A Commentary on the Greek Text* (Grand Rapids, MI: Eerdmans, 1999), 298.

6. Ibid. (emphasis in original).

7. Ibid., 301.

8. Robert H. Mounce, *The Book of Revelation*, rev. ed. (Grand Rapids, MI: Eerdmans, 1998 [1977]), 125–26 (emphasis in original).

9. Jonathan Edwards, "God Glorified in Man's Dependence," in *Sermons and Discourses, 1730–1733*, ed. Mark Valeri (Yale University Press, 1999), 200. The full text of the sermon is found on pp. 200–214.

10. George E. Ladd, *A Commentary on the Revelation of John* (Grand Rapids, MI: Eerdmans, 1976), 66.

11. Jonathan Edwards, "God Glorified in Man's Dependence," 214.

12. John Stott, *What Christ Thinks of the Church* (Grand Rapids, MI: Eerdmans, 1972), 122–23.

13. Much of what follows is adapted from my book *The Singing God* (Orlando: Creation House, 1998), 77–85.

14. Philip Edgcumbe Hughes, *A Commentary on the Epistle to the Hebrews* (Grand Rapids, MI: Eerdmans, 1977), 528.

15. J. I. Packer, *Rediscovering Holiness* (Ann Arbor: Servant Publications, 1992), 215.

16. I've been greatly helped in my understanding of repentance and the explanation that follows by J. I. Packer, *Rediscovering Holiness*, 122–25.

17. Ibid., 123–24 (emphasis in original).

18. Jim Elliff, "The Unrepenting Repenter," http://www.ccwonline.org.

19. Philip Edgcumbe Hughes, *Paul's Second Epistle to the Corinthians* (Grand Rapids, MI: Eerdmans, 1973), 272.

20. J. I. Packer, 138.

21. Colin Hemer, *The Letters to the Seven Churches of Asia in Their Local Setting* (Sheffield: JSOT Press, 1986), 204.

22. John Piper, "How to Buy Gold When You're Broke," a sermon on Rev. 3:14–22, January 2, 1983, http://www.desiringgod.org (emphasis in original).

23. George J. Elvey, "Crown Him with Many Crowns," 1868.